Bill Walkey was born in Birmingham, UK, in 1944 during the second World War. His city was bombed 75 times, almost as badly as London was. His book of short stories speaks of his early childhood and impressions of his devastated surrounding buildings and community, neighbours and family. With a child's perspective during this dark time in history, Bill shares his insights and compassion, so that future generations will better understand the people and places of today.

To my dear grandchildren, Owen, Kaden, Brynja, Talia, Rhys, Ashaya, and Blythe, and to their exceptional parents, Nicola, Shane, and Aunt Demelza.

Bill Walkey

# ESCAPE FROM THE WHITE GHETTO

AUSTIN MACAULEY PUBLISHERS™

LONDON • CAMBRIDGE • NEW YORK • SHARJAH

**Ordering Information**
Quantity sales: Special discounts are available on quantity purchases by corporations, associations, and others. For details, contact the publisher at the address below.

**Publisher's Cataloguing-in-Publication data**
Walkey, Bill
Escape from the White Ghetto

ISBN 9781645756316 (Paperback)
ISBN 9781645756309 (Hardback)
ISBN 9781645756323 (epub e-book)

Library of Congress Control Number: 2022909766

www.austinmacauley.com/us

First Published 2022
Austin Macauley Publishers LLC
40 Wall Street, 33rd Floor, Suite 3302
New York, NY 10005
USA

mail-usa@austinmacauley.com
+1 (646) 5125767

To my loving grandmother, Honor Horton, who raised me to see the world as I do today, and to all the friends who supported completion of my writing, specially, Johanna and Zepa.

# Synopsis

It was 1958. I was 14 years old living in Birmingham, England. Already, I had been bombed by the Luftwaffe while lying in my cot as a new-born at the Sorrento nursing home. I had lived with my Grandparents until I was 5 years old while my parents lived elsewhere, only returning to my parents' home when I was old enough to go to school.

Trying to adjust to the new outside world, and to two new people now introduced as my parents instead of the surrogates I had come to love, I was trying hard to put the pieces together. My parents had moved to the country two years ago from a flat on the main Coventry Road in Small Heath, riding in the back of the moving truck to a beautiful rural area south of Birmingham, only to be jerked back to reality when I was collected by my father from my Grandparents to be brought to a house in Small Heath, a veritable example of Victorian post-industrial revolution slum housing.

As I had walked along the streets from my Grandmother's house to this place, I could not help noticing the squalor, the smoke, the dirty buildings—and last week I had lived in the country with green grass, trees, a little burbling brook, lots of songbirds and fresh air. To look up here was to see the smoky fog and pollution after living in paradise. It seemed my life had been complicated.

Little did I know that the friends I made at this new house would be instrumental in getting me out of here, into a better life—eventually emigrating to Canada and then to Australia.

The problem was that rich and poor in Birmingham looked the same—white. In America, the word ghetto was associated with the socio-depressed races, usually black—you could tell you were in a ghetto by looking at the colour of the skin. If it was black or yellow or brown and the houses looked like the ones around Small Heath, you knew it was a ghetto, but everyone missed the point here that this was a white ghetto!

Poverty, unemployment, poor and decrepit housing, alcoholism, lack of food and social amenities. All the earmarks of any international ghetto, but the incumbents were white and didn't know they were in a ghetto and I was caught in it until I could make good my escape.

The following stories are snippets of life in my white ghetto. Everyday occurrences for the people of Small Heath, but a world away for those outside of the bubble—stories of laughter and sorrow, ups and downs and the way the hardy natives of this district made it until the next day—sometimes!

# 1. Bed Time

Going to bed at night was quite a procedure. In modern times, the kids go to the bathroom, kiss their parents goodnight and that's it until the morning.

In my world, procedures took a slightly different path. When it was decided it was time for me to go to bed, I first had to have a wash. The order of the day was: 'Hands, arms, face and neck!'

Into the kitchen to put a kettle of water on the gas stove to heat up while I went outside to the outdoor toilet.

This was not a tile-lined facility, but rather a brick outhouse with a slate roof and wooden door to block for privacy but open at the top and bottom with a space of about eight inches. The inside walls were whitewashed for cleanliness—oh, and there was a flush toilet, dating back to 1920, with a big rusty cistern at the top of the wall behind the toilet with a pipe down to the back of the toilet pedestal. The flushing worked on the old-fashioned bell system, so flushing water from it became a skill of timing and balance—visitors often spent quite a time trying to get it to work.

Upon leaving the toilet, the first person to bed each night had to pick up the bucket from inside the toilet. This was to serve as the 'potty' during the night in case someone was taken short and didn't want to brave the darkness and outdoor elements.

Returning to the kitchen, a smell of coal gas always greeted you; some from the gas stove and some from the gas leaks that were always present—the water was ready to use.

The kitchen was equipped with only cold water so the water from the tap had to be mixed in an enamel bowl, in the shallow brown stone sink, with the hot water from the kettle; carefully, so that you didn't make it too tepid and lose the warmth. The kitchen was built the same as the toilet: brick walls, painted with whitewash, a slate roof—draughty and two doors opposite each other, one to the yard and one to the entry, both letting draughts in like crazy.

In this euphoric environment it was now time to have a wash in preparation of going to bed.

As there was no heating in the house except for the coal fire in the living room, in the latter part of the day the kitchen was very cold; the brick walls, brick floor and slate roof were not exactly warm and cosy.

Knowing that you couldn't get past the 'inspectors' before you went upstairs to bed, you had no choice but to do 'hands, arms, face and neck.' So, it was a case of O-N-E, T-W-O, T-H-R-E-E and you whipped off your shirt as quickly as you could and dove your hands into the warm water to transfer some of the warmth to your now goose-pimply body!

The three-minute mile may have been something to behold, but washing hands, arms, face, and neck must have been a pretty close second.

The second you were done, it was a case of quick drying on the towel on the hook (still damp from the last use) and back on with the vest and shirt!

Whew, over for another night! Now, past the inspectors and on to bed.

Each night one of our parents would check the cleanliness of our washed parts—sometimes they were rejected and the whole procedure had to be repeated!

Then it was up to bed.

This was the second part of the adventure of bedtime. The stairs were closed in to stop the 'heat' from the living room escaping upstairs and being wasted (?). At the bottom of the stairs was a solid door. When the door was opened the stairs immediately started upwards and made a sharp turn to the right. This meant that if you stood on the left side, there was enough room for your foot, if you stood on the right side there wasn't even enough room for a child's foot as the stair turned so abruptly. This meant that once the door was closed, if you weren't hugging the left side of the stairs and the handrail you could easily slip off the stair and come crashing back into the living room complete with bucket.

As there was no light on the stair, this meant that once the door was closed, you were in complete blackness and you would 'feel' the steps, one by one. Unless you counted the stairs (thirteen in all), you often would reach the top without knowing it and step out for the next step and come crashing down on the top—scaring the life out of you.

Having mounted the stairs, it was a case of feeling your way to your bedroom door in the darkness, a nightly thing, so there was no problem.

The third and final part of the adventure of going to bed would now begin.

Your body was warm, your clothes were warm. The bed was room temperature (freezing cold), your pyjamas were room temperature (freezing cold). The trick was to get your warm body into the cold pyjamas, turn off the light and into the cold bed as quickly as possible to reduce the cold shock into one body-shaking shudder!

This was the next record to the one-minute mile. As you leapt into bed, you curled yourself into a ball to minimise the heat loss from your now shocked body to settle down for a nice warm sleep.

Once in your warm foetal position, you stayed like that all night. Any slight movement of a foot or arm was quickly retracted as the hostile cold surrounds were detected.

Finally, in bed, warm (?) and hoping you didn't have to leave this cocoon to use the bucket on the landing above the stairs. The only other thing that might disturb you was the vibration of the house as a double-decker bus passed your window not six feet away from you on its way to town.

The adventure of bedtime was only eclipsed by the reciprocal of morning rising.

# 2. Going to Market

When I was about sixteen or so, my mother worked for her brother-in-law, a man called Jack Parkes. He had what is known in England as a Greengrocery. This meant he sold fruits, vegetables, chickens and fish. In fact, his sign stated: 'High class fruiterer and fishmonger.'

My uncle, as he was, was a shrewd businessman from whom I learned a lot about business and humankind. He lived in a high-class area of Birmingham called Sutton Coldfield. The people there wanted nothing but the best and for this would pay more.

To get them the best, Uncle Jack would travel to the market area in Birmingham every single morning to buy fresh vegetables, fruit, chickens, crabs and fish. During this time, he had to choose the produce that would be in his shop that day. Facilities for keeping such things over a period of time were inadequate at that time, so it had to be fresh every day.

I took to meeting him there at five o'clock in the morning so that I could go to the market with him and then go back to his shop in Sutton and work there for the day. My reward for this was five shillings (the equivalent today of about fifty cents). It was hard work, but I enjoyed it so much and I learned a lot. It was Uncle Jack and this market environment that taught me how to barter, haggle and get good deals. Uncle Jack taught me that when the money is in your pocket you can do and say what you like and the vendors will still be nice to you—they want your money. Once it's in their pockets, they won't give you a flea to breed off and this was true.

He taught me how to check apples and vegetables to see they were fresh and in good condition, check celery to see if it was limp celery that had been 'doctored' and how to reject anything that doesn't come up to standard. As he said, a fool and his money are soon parted, but he was no fool and didn't part with anything until he was sure of what he was buying. The marketeers soon knew they could not pull anything off on him and ceased to try. They looked a little askance at my appearance wondering who I was.

It was understood that a lot of what was sold at the early morning market was not there legally or legitimately and so a quick bargain on some things was a sure way of getting rid of it, pocketing the cash and making a quick exit. A new face, like mine, was often treated with suspicion in case I was an undercover policeman.

The main market was on Jamaica Row and was a hustling, bustling, noisy place right in the heart of Birmingham, behind St. Martin's Church. It was a huge, spacious, red-brick Victorian building with high roofing and lots of room inside for all the piles of boxes and stalls the noisy marketers set up even before we arrived there. The high, garage-like doors reached up to the top of the high walls like the gates of a fortress. Inside, the well-worn cobblestones had been witness to such markets since the beginning of the previous century.

In many ways, it reminded me of a typical den of iniquity. You knew that everyone there was out to make money. Everyone knew it, everyone did it and everyone didn't hide the fact and if they could get away with a little extra—well that was fair game.

There was lots of haggling, shouting, lots of pseudo-annoyance if the price countered was too low. But everyone knew where the margins were and even allowing for a sensible profit—it was still a cat and mouse game. By the time the average citizen was on the street at nine o'clock, fortunes had to be made or lost before the goods spoiled!

In those days, when it was time for bananas, they had to be shipped to Britain while they were still green and unripe. Close to the market was a special building that had an area similar to a gas furnace. The bananas, which had arrived in long, heavy boxes—about five feet long and a foot square at the end—packed in straw, were put into the 'furnace' to add heat to the bananas. This was an instant ripening procedure. Quite often, when you went to pick up your bananas, they weren't quite 'ripe' enough. This meant you had to go away and come back a little later.

If we had made our purchases and our bananas weren't ripe, it meant we had to do something until they were. Uncle Jack would pay the various marketeers, always in cash and tell them where his van was parked. Each of the marketeers had a few porters. These young swarthy guys would load the various produce items onto their carts and deliver it to your vehicle. The carts were quite unique in their appearance; two large steel-rimmed wheels clanking along at the front, a flat deck on top of the wheels and two handles to push it along—something like a Chinese rickshaw in reverse.

It was a work of art to see them rushing along as they pushed these carts, loaded to the sky, twisting and turning through the congested alleyways of produce, cars, vans and narrow streets to get to your vehicle. In all the time I did this, I never saw them scratch a car or lose even an apple off the load—they were masters at their trade. They would deliver to the vehicle, which was unlocked, and then rush to where Uncle Jack was to tell him they had delivered it—a tip was always waiting—and then on to the next load.

So where did we go while we were waiting? This whole area of Birmingham thrived on selling and markets. It was no wonder that on every corner, alcove or twist in the road was a cafe. Not just an ordinary cafe, but more like a trucker's cafe. The hub-bub of the exuberant marketers and buyers boasting about their steals or sales, the clinking of the metal spoons against the mugs as the customers quickly stirred their cups of tea to mix the milk and sugar before gulping it down with a mouthful of hot toast and jam. Here the tea was thick and strong, delivered in mugs, not teacups and the toast was black—on one side anyway (it had been done under the grill, not in a toaster)—heaped up with jam or marmalade.

So with a cup of thick tea in one hand and a thick wedge of black toast and jam in the other—what more could a man ask for at 4:30 in the morning? There was no time to sit and relish the welcome tastes on a cold, windy morning, just enough time to swill the toast with the tea, drain the dregs and off we go!

When we knew our bananas were ready, we would gulp down the tea and head for the banana shed with the remnants of the sticky toast clenched in our fists.

The ride to Sutton was a long one, so I would often fall asleep, looking forward to serving in the store and learning more about how to clean chickens to make thin ones look fat, fat ones look fatter and fillet halibut without leaving a scrap on the bones—oh, life was so good!

# 3. Coal Lady

Old lady White, as she was known, was the local coal lady. She lived a few doors up from my family on Cattell Road. Every few weeks, she would appear in the road with a truckload of coal in one-hundredweight (112 lbs.) sacks. She had given up her cart and horse and now hired a driver and his truck at the rail sidings where she bought the coal. The driver was usually a different man each time but always the same outfit. It was customary for a coal man to wear a leather cap whose peak was turned to the back of the head to protect his neck from the rough material of the coal sack. The sacks were thick, heavy and dirty hemp sacks that were durable and showed the wear of many years. Over his shirt, the coal man always wore a smooth, leather vest. I thought the leather always looked the same as the leather he had seen on horses' harness. This protected his clothes and back. It really didn't do much to protect his clothes because the man's face and hands were always so black with coal dust. I wondered how on earth he ever got them clean when he got home at night. To protect their feet from wayward sacks, the coal men wore big leather boots, also black. It was one of these men that Mrs. White always brought with her. She would walk from house to house ahead of the truck and knock on the door. "Coal today, Missus?" she would ask. "How much?" was the usual reply.

"I've got top grade coal today, none of the rubbish, at six shillings and sixpence, or anthracite at seven and four pence."

"What?" my mother would reply, "Last time it was only five and ten pence!"

"Coal's gone up in price since then," Lady White would counter, "that's the best I can do."

"O.K., give me two hundredweights."

The bartering-quibbling was a customary exchange expected by both. Lady White would write out a receipt and give it to my mother in exchange for the cash.

"Two bags here!" Lady White would yell to the driver and then move on to the next house.

My mother always took two bags whatever the price was and whenever Lady White came so she was regarded as a regular customer. One day, my mother was out when it was coal day. Lady White would leave the coal anyway and stuff the invoice in the crack of the back door. When my mother arrived home, she sent me with the money to pay Mrs. White. I didn't really like going to her house but I knew better than to refuse. The entry to her house seemed extra dark. Maybe it was the tree that grew at the end of her entry that blocked out the light, but it was eerie. I quietly knocked on the back door of Mrs. White's house. I knocked quietly hoping she wouldn't hear if she was there and then he could honestly leave saying he had got no answer.

"Who's there?" came a voice.

*Oh, no,* I thought, *she's home.*

"It's me!" I called back.

"Who's me? Come in any way!" was the reply from inside the house.

I opened the door very slowly. Hanging over the doorway behind the door to stop drafts was a thick curtain. I had to push the heavy curtain away to get through the doorway. As I struggled free of the heavy material it fell back into place, blotting out the doorway entirely.

*I'm trapped!* I thought, making my way through the kitchen I had stepped in toward the living room door.

I stopped at the closed door and politely knocked again. "Come in! Come in! I won't bite you!" Mrs. White seemed to sound impatient.

I stepped into the living room. It was dim inside with only an oil lamp for light. The yellow light from the glass mantle gave the room an eerie appearance as it flickered in the draught from the door.

*Why doesn't she turn the light on*? I wondered to myself, and then noticed there was no sign of an electric light anywhere.

Mrs. White sat on a couch behind a low table on which there were a pile of invoices and receipts just like the one I had in my hand. My mother had sent me with invoice and money with instructions to make sure Mrs. White signed to say she'd had the money. Mrs. White took the money from me and began to write something on the paper I had handed her. I cast a quick, furtive glance around the room. I'd never seen a room like this before. Where the fireplace was in his house was a huge, old-fashioned Victorian range. I had seen ranges before, but never like this. It had a big oven on the left-hand side, drawers on the right, but what caught my eye

22

was the brass rail that ran the whole length of the mantle-piece. From the rail hung a chain with large, brass links. At the end of the chain was a big, black cauldron that was suspended over the open coals from the chain. Something was cooking in the cauldron, I could hear it bubbling. I had only seen such cauldrons in pictures of witches and wizards. I was getting worried and wanted out of there. At the front of the fireplace there were three or four thick iron bars that held the coal in the grate. To the side of these bars was a circular platform, on the end of an arm that could swing the platform close to the fire or completely away from it. The platform was currently sitting close to the fire and there was a black kettle sitting on it with steam coming from the spout. The fire looked very nice and rosy red and cast a warm glow over all of the hearth and its surrounding fender. The fender of metal and wood stopped any coal or cinders that happened to fall out of the fire from rolling onto the floor or adjacent carpet. I noticed that the grate had been recently black-leaded and shone in the firelight. The tile of the hearth had also been done recently as it was still nice and red without any scuffmarks or black from the coal. I thought that for a strange old lady, she certainly kept her house nice. My gaze had wandered onto the long thick drapes that covered the living room window. They were thick, red drapes, rather like the one over the back door, but these had tassels. They hung from large brass curtain rings in a long pole that extended past the width of the window. The ends of the pole had decorated swirls on them that gave the whole window a decorative flair. Before my eyes could wander any more, I was brought back to reality by Mrs. White's shrill voice.

"What are you staring at? Don't you know it's rude to stare? Here give this to your mother, and get yourself home!" Mrs. White shoved a piece of paper into my hand, which I presumed to be the receipt.

I didn't need any second bidding. I was out of the house like a shot. I stood at the end of her yard and looked back at her house. It gave me the creeps just to be in her yard. I ran down her entry into the relative safety of the street and then ran all the way home. I hoped that next time old lady White called with coal, my mother would be home.

# 4. Ghetto

The part of Small Heath where I lived was an industrialist's dream. A rich source of cheap, generally unskilled labour where the main concern of any of its occupants was a day's work, a roof over the head and a pub on every corner to satisfy a thirst after a hard day's work. Aspiration of the mass consisted of a good sleep at night, a wife to keep you warm and cook your Sunday dinner and clean, dry socks to go to work with the next morning. There was never any thought of bettering oneself and rising out of this Victorian brick jungle. Those who showed any sign of doing better than the man next door were quickly subdued by taunts and family pressure. To show a better side or inclination of improving one's lot would be met by ostracism by one's fellow workers and neighbours.

The adventurer would be soon told, "Who do you think you are with your airs and graces?"

Even to show up in the road with a new car or a colour television would ensure comments such as, "He's getting a bit above himself, isn't he?"

Progress in the area was self-limiting by such peers and as such ensured that the labour force stayed at a manageable level of subordination which suited the local industrialist well. He knew that he would not get any trouble from workers such as these. With a strong foreman on the job, requests for pay raises or holidays would be unheard of. No one wanted to be the maverick in an area like this. The pal at your elbow, leaning on the bar in the local pub was the ultimate after a day's work. No working man worth his salt wanted to lose that and so the status quo remained the same generation after generation—and men were proud to say so. One of the bi-products of such an infrastructure, was to see young children hanging on the pub doors at lunchtime calling to their mothers inside for money for chips or other fast foods to satisfy their hunger until the evening meal. Often the wailing at the door was met with a back hander for bothering the parent or worse still; a total denial of sustenance as the mother would claim.

"Where do you think I've got money for lunches from the store, do you think money grows on trees?"

This alcohol induced answer still did not answer the fact that the child went back to school hungry and not for the first time. In this rabbit warren of congested living—narrow, congested streets of old, dirty brick houses built so close together and so many in a small area—there thrived a life of resilient, hardworking people. Some terrace back houses were so congested around a small yard that there were two entrances to the yard, in case of fire. These were called 'double knacks.' As soon as someone said they lived on a double knack, it was understood that their living quarters were of the lowest denomination, in an area where the normal was considered slum. Inside the houses were not to be found dining room sets, or bedroom sets or even a set of dishes. A simple description of the inside of a typical

Small Heath house was to call it 'Early Poverty.' The sad thing was that the early poverty lasted until late in life. There was no escape! Life in Small Heath consisted of a hand-to-mouth existence. A mother did her best to get from day-to-day and feed her family the best way she could. There were no fancy or new clothes, especially for the mother. The father would occasionally need new boots for work. These could be acquired through the benevolence of the Daily Mail newspaper who ran a non-profit society to help such bread winners get to work and back safely. Clothes were passed down the family as the older children grew out of them, and when this system broke down the clothes were often recycled from the kids next door. Unfortunately, if you were a younger child, all you saw were ragged, resewn and recycled clothes. This did little for self-worth or pride, but it kept you warm in the day and warm at night when you had to cuddle up to your siblings to keep warm in a cold house—bed clothes sometimes consisted of Dad's old overcoat from last winter. Dirt, lice and nits were prevalent. Dirty faces at school and in the street were a common sight. The only thing pristine in this wilderness of sadness and poverty was the pride of the people who lived there. They may have been poor, they may have been unwashed, they may not have had much money, but they had lots of personal pride in what little things they did have. To match this they were honest, straightforward and would help anyone worse off than they were at a minute's notice. The whole area was always immersed in hazy smoke, either from the factory chimneys or the multitude of coal fires burning in the grates of the houses. In the fall of the year, the low clouds and foggy atmosphere joined forces with the smoke of the area to form what is now known as smog. This yellow-brown mass would swirl along the sidewalk ahead of large vehicles such as buses or trucks and show up in their headlights like some cotton candy monster from another planet. Smaller vehicles would follow closely behind these larger vehicles as the latter were equipped with large, orange fog lights that would peer through the mess and permit a little observation into the road ahead. Often, the conductor of the bus would walk ahead to confirm there was a clear space ahead so that the driver would not run into a stalled off abandoned vehicle sitting in the road. Anyone caught out in this mess would arrive home with a dirty 'V' shape on their shirts where the top coat had left this part of the shirt exposed. Upon entering buildings, people were convinced that the fog was excluded from the house as it was easy to see things in the living rooms. They seemed unconvinced that there was as much smog in their houses as there was in the street. At this time in the history of Small Heath, all of the natives were white, English and proud of their ancestry. The local dialect was a hard, nasal mix made up from the Roman/ French/ Celtic/ Nordic races that had ranged over the area during its volatile history. The Mercian line, where all of these races had decided to call it quits, ran close to Small Heath and hence the creole mix of words and dialects. This dialect was very strong and identifiable with the area and prevented many would-be businessmen from climbing the executive ladder in large companies. They preferred the polished Oxford type dialect for their image and shunned the midland 'working-class' scholar. Even at the age of nine, I could tell the difference after living with my Grandparents for so long.

I realised that my parents, in their uncaring ignorance, had walked my family into a social trap from which we might never be able to escape. This prison didn't have bars, far worse, every person around them was a jailer committed to making sure no one escaped into the other world outside Small Heath. This was a life sentence, and my parents were willing inmates. I felt that moving into Small Heath was similar to a sea bird swimming toward the slick of a sinking oil tanker. As the bird moved closer for a better look, the fingers of the spreading oil reached out and immersed the unsuspecting curiosity. No matter how the bird wriggled, squirmed of fought against it, the environment slowly engulfed the unwilling victim and would forever change what had been a pristine subject. No matter how much anyone tried to clean the bird afterwards, it would always show its stains of its encounter. If only the bird had been prevented from approaching the slick, it would never have had to consider fighting free from such a destructive force. This was the impression I had the day my father walked me from the bus to my oil slick in Cattell Road. If only I had had the forethought to have stayed with my Grandparents. It was too late. I had asked to be with my parents. I had got what I asked for and must now ride my Titanic. This place was not like the place called Harlem in America I had heard about on the radio, but I knew for a fact that it was equally as much a ghetto as any in the world. As we approached the front of the 'new' house, I noticed the two little stone steps up to the front door, worn into a concave dip from years and years of use by the countless feet of time gone by. As this was the only entrance I could see, I headed for it. Instead of following me, my father walked into the tunnel-shaped entrance at the side of the doorway. I did not want to be left standing on the front step so I quickly followed him into the brick tunnel that led toward the back of the house. I had never been into one of these types of entries. As you went into it, it was so long that it seemed like a long, brick tube. Underfoot, the entry had blue brick; a very hard form of brick specifically made for hard-wear areas. Part way up the entry in the right-hand side of the wall was a narrow, black door. The doorknob was higher up than usual giving the door the appearance of a factory door I had seen many times before in local factories. I watched as my father inserted what looked like an old-fashioned dungeon-type key that made a grinding sound as it was turned in the lock. It swung open to reveal we were standing in the kitchen. This was not like my Nan's kitchen. This kitchen was dirty. Against the far wall, was an old Victorian range with its warming oven, an arm that swung over the open fire on which a pot could be hung and hot plates on top. The whole thing was covered in ashes that had obviously been there for a long time, giving it a very eerie, abandoned look. Next to it was a copper boiler in similar condition. The hemispherical boiler sat over a small fire pit that was used to heat the water in the copper for washing, bathing or any other use hot water could be put to. Completing a trio next to the copper was the sink. This was no ordinary sink but a real-life genuine relic of the 1880s. Rectangular in shape of brown stone and about six inches deep. The brown colour alone gave it a very unsanitary look, a peek into it confirmed the first suspicion. Its only water source was a cold-water tap fed by a led pipe that has been repaired so many times there was very little of the original left. The width of the kitchen reached only half way across the width of the house so that there was a small yard running alongside the kitchen accessed by a door opposite the one they had just come through. A turn to the right and up a small step brought them into what seemed to be the living room. It was decorated in pre-war style with vertical boarding half way up the walls in government surplus colours of brown and cream. The only grace the room had was an open coal fireplace with a tiled facing. A single electric bulb hung from its wire in the middle of the ceiling. I was pleased to see my mother who was kneeling at the foot of the stairs with a pail of caustic soda at her side and a scrubbing brush in her hand.

"Hello, Mommy, what are you doing? I asked.

"Don't step on the stairs, they're still wet! She replied, "I'm scrubbing the filth off them, they're disgusting! Don't lean against the wall in your good clothes there's dirt everywhere!"

I had hoped for a little better greeting from my mother but by now such expectations had diminished—this was normal. My mother was more concerned about her scrubbing and her stairs than how I was. At least my Nan always stopped what she was doing to speak to me or at least show some interest. Even my Grandad would put down his racing form to see what I wanted, and I knew how important it was that Barney the Bookie got his piece of paper. No hug, no kiss, no nothing. Ah well. All my mother seemed concerned about was whether or not she'd have to wash my clothes. So I decided I would explore the house. I wanted to see what was in the front room so I moved toward it and my father followed me. There was an old door to the front room that had originally had panes of glass in it. They were now painted out to give the door an opaque appearance. The lock on the door had ceased to work many years ago and the door was now held closed by a long hasp hook that had to be unlatched to allow access to the room. Then we stepped into the room, I could see it was much the way it must have been when the house was built. Huge, folding, wooden shutters stood on the face of the bay window. I thought they were more to keep the draft out rather that the light. The high ungainly dinosaurs threatened to fall if any attempt was made to open them. I gave them a shove. They just groaned, the hinges made a grating noise but did not budge.

"Don't touch them, they're unsafe," my father warned, "Keep well away from them or you'll have your mother after you if you get dirty."

The only other things in the room besides the shutters was a fireplace, a cupboard and a fortress-type front door complete with an even larger dungeon-type key that I was never able to turn in its rusted housing. As I left the room to go back into the living room where my mother was still labouring on the stairs, I noticed a small pane of glass in the wall adjacent to the living room. I crossed the small dividing hallway area between the front room and the living room. This passage area accommodated on the left, a pantry, and on the right, the door to the cellar. Back in the living room, I noticed that in the living room wall adjacent to the front room was another of those panes of glass. They were strategically placed in the two walls so that an adult could look through them and see the front door. I found out later that this was a method used by householders who had turned their front rooms into shops to look into their front-room come-store and see if they had any customers without actually having to leave their living room. I then realised that this was why the panes of glass in the door to the front room had been painted out; so that the people sitting in the living room would have privacy from anyone entering the former shop. Looking through these two panes of glass, the observer was unaware of the actual space between the walls as this space was in darkness. Such family shops sprung up all over the place in front rooms as the whims of people took fancy to do so. Such things as permits and by-laws did not exist. These stores were referred to as 'uxta' stores by the local people. The word was probably derived from an old English work 'huxter' dating back to the word 'hawker' or seller.

# 5. Alone at 45

It was a Saturday, not long after I had gone to live back with my parents in their new home on Coventry Road in Small Heath, and we were on our way to visit my Grandparents in Alum Rock.

To me it was like a homecoming. I had spent so much of my young life there before finally going back to my parents' house when they finally secured a council house, or actually, flat.

We had to take two buses to get there, so by the time we arrived outside 45 Brookhill Road it was already getting dark; I guess it must have been in the fall or early winter.

The front door had a big knocker, which sat over the letterbox opening. It had originally been a brass one my Grandfather had cast, but when the vogue became chrome, it had been chromed and sat atop the letterbox in all its glory.

It had always made a loud noise when I had been on the inside when someone came, so I was careful not to bang too hard, just two taps.

In a very short while, my Uncle Bert came to the summons and opened the door.

"What's wrong with the back door, too far for you?" he asked a little irritably, "Next time use the back!"

I knew he must have been watching sports on his television, he never liked being disturbed from that.

"Sorry, Uncle Bert," I offered.

He just looked at me the way uncles look at their nephews when they didn't really mean to be mean. He disappeared into the living room to watch his soccer and left me to close the door behind myself.

I had run ahead of my parents. I knew they would use the entry to the back door, so I didn't have to wait with the door open for them.

I was happy to see my Uncle Bert again; he had always been very kind to me when I had lived there. On Saturday nights, when we watched the 'telly,' he would often offer me a sip of his Guinness—just from that I knew I was special to him, he never shared his Guinness with anyone!

My parents arrived soon after and asked my Uncle, "Where's Mom and Dad?"

"Upstairs getting ready," Uncle Bert responded.

Just then, I heard my grandfather's rather irritated voice, "How long, Honor?"

My grandfather was obviously annoyed that my grandmother was taking so long in the bathroom. He was a very patient man, but when his Saturday night dominoes game was being delayed by a woman doing who knows what for how long in the bathroom, patience became a little thin.

I very soon afterward heard my grandmother's footsteps across the landing signifying her passage to the bedroom and the open bathroom door for my grandfather's ablutions.

They were soon downstairs looking spiffy and smart and ready to take on the town. It seemed a shame to me even as a young person, that all this fuss was simply to go down to the Brookhill pub at the bottom of the road to have a drink of beer, or maybe many drinks of beer.

I didn't mind. After all, I would be spending a nice evening with Uncle Bert watching his television and having fun laughing with him like we always used to do on Saturday nights when I lived there.

As I was getting ready for this evening of fun and TV, my world was blown apart.

"Bert!" My mother turned to Uncle Bert, "Why don't you come down for a drink with us, you haven't been out for quite a while?"

I waited for the perfunctory reply of, 'No thanks, I'll just stay home and watch the telly.'

To my surprise and personal horror, he replied, "Now, that's an idea, just wait a minute and I'll get my coat on."

"But, but, but, what about me?" I half asked, half choked, "Who's going to stay with me?"

"Oh, you'll be alright by yourself for half an hour," my mother replied as she brushed off my obvious concern in her attempt to reach the front door without having to spend too much time explaining.

*Half an hour,* I thought.

I knew what these sorties to the pub were like! They wouldn't be back until the pub closed at ten o'clock, four or more hours from now!

I was quickly sat down with a drink of orange juice and a biscuit, told not to worry.

The suction of bodies leaving the room was like a vacuum cleaner as they all headed for the front door with final, "We won't be long!"

This I didn't believe. I sat very quietly in my Grandfather's chair—juice in one hand, biscuit in the other. By the time they had left, it was already dark outside so they had flipped the living room light on and closed the living room door behind them.

There I sat. And I sat and I sat.

My juice was gone, my biscuit was gone—there was nothing moving except my pulse and heartbeat. All of a sudden, this house that I had lived in for so many years became a huge mansion full of hidden horrors.

My Grandparents and Uncle Bert had been very kind to me when I had lived there, but up till now there had always been someone there, at least one person. Now I was sitting in this empty house, all by myself, with mixed memories of good and bad.

This was the only room with a light on, and who knows what lay in the shadows under the big dining room table or those funny sounds I had heard under Uncle Bert's bed, and the noises under Auntie Leah's bed when you sat on them— what really was it that made those noises.

Up to now it didn't matter, because one of them was always there if something did jump out and grab you.

There was no central heating in the houses in those days. As the coal fire went down, it needed stoking up. I looked around for the coalscuttle, trying to keep very still and not give my position away in case someone was looking through the French door that didn't have curtains to it.

The scuttle was empty. Oh, what was I to do. The pile of coal was out in the yard against the fence; the dark yard, no light.

It would mean I would have to open the big back door, go out by myself into the blackened yard and get the coal. I knew exactly where the coal was, I had been there so many times but there was always someone holding the door open so that the light shone on the coal.

I was not going outside to get coal.

The room started to get colder and colder—I started to shiver. My coat was on the back of the chair by the door. The more I thought about moving to get it, the more I became terrified with what could happen to me if I did.

I was scared to death. In all the years I had been in this house, I had never been alone.

Now I was alone, and very scared.

There was a falling, scratching sound from the pantry right opposite where I sat.

I froze in my chair. There it was again! I wondered who was hiding in the pantry. It was so loud it must be someone hiding in there waiting to get me when I went near the door to get my coat!

As I watched the doorknob to see if it turned, there was a sound from the room above me. It was the sound Auntie's bed made when she sat up in bed when she woke up in the morning.

But she isn't here! Who made that sound?

I heard the sound of coal falling in the yard where the coal was piled. Oh no.

By now I was frozen to the spot. Afraid to be where I was, afraid to move. I needed to go to the bathroom, but there was no way I was going into the dark hallway to go up the dark stairs to a dark bathroom where there were sounds coming from the adjacent rooms.

I started to cry and cry and cry, until I thought I would break apart with crying and sobbing—my body was shaking so much. I cried so much my nose began to run but I was too scared to put my hand in my pocket and get my handkerchief.

The green candles ran down my top lip, two of them, and into my mouth. It was the grossest thing I could imagine and tasted awful but now the creaks and groans were coming more often and I was totally convinced the house was full of demons out to get me.

My eyes were sore from crying, my nose was running all over the place, my cheeks hurt from crying so hard and no matter how I cried no one came to my aid. By now, I needed to pee so badly my bladder was at the point of exploding but I was not leaving this chair.

Where was everyone? Why hadn't they come back? They had been away nearly three hours. I had watched and timed their absence by the clock on the shelf that just looked back at me and went tick tock, tick tock.

At every quarter of the hour it would boom out its chimes, scaring me even more.

I was getting to the point that I had cried so much, there was no cry left, just aching cheeks. I was also at the point of peeing in my pants.

Just when I thought the end of the world was coming, I heard that wonderful, welcome sound of Granddad's key going into the Yale lock of the front door. It was a sound like heaven itself. He was always the first to come home.

I felt this surge of relief, similar I would venture, to shipwrecked sailors who are clinging to flotsam when the coastguard cutter comes alongside to save them from certain death.

Granddad came into the room and took an immediate look at the sorry plight of his favourite grandson. He knew right away what was wrong and why—Granddad always did.

"Come on, my son," he said, holding out his arms, "Come to Granddad."

He scooped me up and hugged me to him.

"Do you mean to tell me your mom and dad haven't been back to see you in all this time?"

"No," I choked out, "And I need to go to the toilet, really badly."

Granddad took me up to the bathroom and after I had emptied a rather relieved bladder I washed my face with cold water to hide my crying.

He was a very quiet man and didn't speak out loud very much, but I knew my parents were going to hear about this, whether they liked it or not.

During the time in the bathroom, I had heard others come into the house below me.

"Are you alright now?" Granddad asked and when I smiled at him he opened the door for me to go downstairs.

When I opened the door to go into the living room, the adults were preoccupied with cups of tea and sandwiches of cheese and onion and didn't even look my way.

Finally, my mother acknowledged my presence by, "Oh, there you are, we wondered where you were."

I was so glad to have people around me. The noises in the pantry and the rooms above had disappeared, and someone had gone to get coal and the fire was burning nicely.

My parents had stood up and were putting their coats on and heading for the door. I was so pleased to be going home, I had had enough sadness, strange noises and hobgoblins for one night. At least in a little while I would be in my own bed with my own familiar things.

My parents saw me make a move to get my coat off the back of the chair.

"Oh no, you're not coming with us tonight. The all-night service on the buses has finished and it's so late so we will have to walk home. You're staying here. Someone will pick you up tomorrow, or maybe your Aunt will bring you home. If not, well, your Nan won't mind keeping you until next weekend."

# 6. Chicken Feed

In the flat we lived in on Coventry Road, it was the second and third stories of an old Victorian house. The whole house was by itself quite big and impressive. It had been divided in the main entrance hall.

The door to our house started at the bottom of the stairs that went upstairs to the bedrooms, and the door to the downstairs part of the house started at the beginning of the passage that went to the front room, the lower rooms and kitchen of the original house.

The front door itself was a big, solid wooden door with lots of ornamentation on it, approached by a magnificent set of stone steps. To access the house, one had to pass through an iron gate, typical of Victorian era houses, up a curving path overlooked by a large, spreading tree.

The splitting of the house into two flats had obviously been because of economic reasons of income support, but it was sad that such a beautiful Victorian house had to end its days as two flats.

Our flat had originally had three bedrooms; one at the front of the house, one in the middle, a toilet, and a back bedroom. The typical long passageway joined the front two bedrooms and toilet—Victorian homes were famous for their passageways. At the toilet, the passage turned left abruptly which brought you to the top of the stairs on the left and a short passage to the right which led to the back bedroom.

The only other feature to this layout was a steep stairway from the passageway at the junction of the two front bedrooms. This stairway led upwards to the attic. In most homes this would have been the storage area. It did not boast bedroom-like finishing. Rather the opposite— vaulted-structured 'ceilings' which were actually the sloping beams of the roof structure, a bare wooden floor and a light consisting of a bulb holder hanging on the end of a long wire cord.

The dark brown colour of the wood had not been painted but retained the aged look of unfinished wood and a small window in the roof to give light to the room. This was my bedroom. The only things in it were my bed and my brother's bed. Two iron framed beds with wire bed 'springs' and flock mattresses. No wardrobe—our clothes hung over the end of the bed, no side tables, no nothing. This is what we climbed the stairs to every night when it was time to go to bed.

It was a time of post-war austerity and I, with my brother, were main contributors. The larger front bedroom was sublet to my Aunt and Uncle and their baby, my cousin.

As our family lived on the 'bedroom' floor, the bedroom at the back of the house had been turned into a kitchen. The back bedroom-come-kitchen still retained its cast-iron fireplace and grate in the back wall. This was the only form of heating for us, so we had to keep a coal fire going in it to warm the room.

Besides this, it had a sink, a draining board and a little cupboard to the side of our exit door from the kitchen. Other than an old wooden scrub-top table and chairs, the room did not boast any other refinements.

Our exit door from the kitchen was not a true back door, rather the fire escape that the local council had obviously insisted on when the house was converted into flats. This was our 'deck.'

The door, on the yard wall, led onto a fire escape platform which measured about four feet by eight. It had wooden rails around the top and steep, wooden stairs down to the yard below. For safety's sake, the surround of the deck had mesh wire around the perimeter and a latched gate at the top of the stairs.

This was my recreation area and where I would occasionally get exposure to fresh air. Not much to boast about but at six years of age it seemed good, and it was all there was.

Down below the deck was a typical Victorian blue-brick yard. These blue bricks were as hard as steel and almost impossible to break, even intentionally. Beyond this was an unkempt yard consisting of mostly dirt, a little grass and a few weeds; quite a barren place when I come to think of it.

The ubiquitous red brick walls defined both sides of the back garden, with blue-brick crest bricks designed to keep the weather from eroding the wall structure. The one on the right was intact and complete. The one on the left had a breach in it over which Convolvulus (Morning Glory) grew. When I asked once why the wall was broken, I was told a bomb (from WWII) had done it.

At the bottom of the garden was the end (side) wall of the house that ran at right angles to our row of houses. It had at some time been plastered. A common occurrence if the bricks had become porous, or had cracked from bomb damage. As our house was opposite the Singer motor works, which had produced war materials, it is probable it was because of the latter.

The whole back garden sloped up from the yard to the plastered house. In rainy times, this meant a downhill flow of mud and water. The erosion over time had worn a groove from the top of the garden to the yard. In later times, a wall was constructed at the junction of the yard and garden to retard this action.

After the war, the Anderson shelters that were used as air raid shelters were everywhere and unwanted. They were converted into garages, lean-tos and as in our case, a chicken pen.

Our chicken pen supported about six to eight chickens, I can't remember quite how many. As money was very scarce in those times, I can only assume that my Grandfather had given them to my parents.

I was never allowed to play in our yard or even do what children do in the garden. I was a lofty 'prisoner' on my eyrie deck suspended above the blue-brick yard.

One day, my mother asked me to go and feed the chickens. This was great news to me—to be able to leave the deck and go up the garden by myself—a rare treat not to be missed!

My mother gave me the bag of chicken corn in a small paper bag. She told me to give them 'just a bit, not too much.' How much is that I wondered. Instead of giving me 'just a bit' in another bag or cup or whatever, I was given the whole bag.

I set off on my journey to the top of the garden and the chickens. Chickens, being what chickens are, showed how excited they were to see me, especially when I threw the first handful of corn through the wire into their run. They were so excited and pleased at my offering—I threw them another handful. As I found out in later life, chickens are basically brainless and reactive, responding to the last stimulus they receive.

In my young mind these chickens seemed very hungry—reacting after every handful, and handful, and handful.

I pondered on just how much this 'just a bit' was when I noticed that the original full bag of corn was now only the size of my fist—a six-year-old's fist. Oops! I wound the bag down to the remaining amount of corn and decided it was time to return to the house.

When I walked into the kitchen, very pleased with my handling of the chicken feeding, my obvious optimism was greeted with a look of horror and red-faced anger of my mother.

"What have you done?' She demanded angrily.

"I fed the chickens," I replied, pleased with my first solo action into our great back yard.

"I said just a bit," my mother thundered.

I couldn't quite understand this rage and anger when I had done what I thought was a great job of feeding the chickens.

"Do you know how much that stuff costs?" she demanded still raging at me with obvious vocal anger.

She grabbed hold of me, hauled me against her and began to slap my rear so hard with her hand (a very strong, muscled hand I might add) that I felt pain I had never known before. In all the time I had lived with my Grandparents, they had never hit me like this. They had been angry with me sometimes, but never beaten me physically like my own mother was now doing.

Finally, she flung me away from her and ordered me up to my bedroom.

"And you can stay there until your father comes home, then we'll see what he has to say! And don't come down, you're not getting any dinner (supper-evening meal)."

I fled to my bedroom afraid of my mother's anger, and even more intimidated and afraid of what supplemental punishment I would get when my father came home.

I sat on the edge of my bed in the attic bedroom, head in my hands and cried, and cried, and cried.

I cried so much, I finally didn't have any more tears to cry. From crying, or sheer exhaustion, I finally fell asleep on my bed.

I was awakened by the gruff voice of my father greeting my mother as he arrived home, and the heavy footsteps as he climbed the flight of stairs from the entrance hall to the kitchen level.

I sat there terrified, somehow waiting for the steps to continue up the second flight of stair to my attic bedroom. I heard his footsteps instead going down the passageway to the kitchen and the sound of the kitchen door closing behind my father as he went into the kitchen.

I heard the muffled voices of my mother and father in the kitchen and sat there in trepidation wondering what my fate was going to be.

After what seemed to be like an eternity, I heard my mother coming from the kitchen and up the attic stairs.

I sat there wondering what was going to happen.

The door opened slowly, letting light from the skylight over the stairs into my dimly lit room.

She had with her a tray with a sandwich and a cup of milk on it.

"Here you are," she said passing the tray to me.

"I haven't said anything to your father because I know he would be mad," she said and left the same way she had come.

I ate my offering, realised I was not leaving my room until school time tomorrow, undressed and climbed into bed, just still trying to work out in my mind why a special day feeding the chickens had turned out to be such a horrendous calamity.

# 7. The Boy at the Coal Yard

Sometimes, winter in Birmingham would come early with a vengeance and no one would be ready no matter how many years before it had happened.

This meant that money being short as it was after the WWII, there was never any 'extra' put aside for the unseen things like an early winter.

The result was the usual panic and 'who would have thought it' attitude. One of the things always missing was enough coal to keep the living room warm and the damp out of the house.

As 'Lady' White, the coal lady, came on a regular, scheduled agenda, there was nothing to do but go to the local coal yard if you were out of coal and pay the inflated prices to get a little coal until Lady White appeared with her budget coal. Many times this 'budget' coal was the hard, shiny coal which had little or no heating property at all. It was mixed in with the good coal as a way to debase and cheapen a bag of coal and in doing so, make it affordable to the local residents.

The coal yard was opposite the Atlas pub at the junction of Garrison Lane and Cattell Road. In typical rip-off style, the only access to the coal yard was through two big wooden gates, locked at night with a big iron chain and a padlock. The actual 'yard' was nothing more than the space left between two buildings after construction of the housing block. The builders never cooperated to end up with a continuous line of houses; they were only interested in finishing their building, getting their money and getting out before the leaks showed. For this reason, there were many of these 'yards' utilised by coal merchants, used car sellers and the like.

The high brick-end wall of the two blocks provided a simple high security place for the likes of these coal merchants who only had to add the high gates and the padlock.

The coal yard opposite the Atlas Pub was one of these typical yards. There was always the 'boss,' and usually two or three of his henchmen, who were there to control the proceedings and make sure no one tried to leave without paying. These henchmen were typical 'bully boys' who were the epitome of social insecurity, who couldn't or wouldn't get any other work anywhere else. They enjoyed terrorizing older ladies or old men as well as little boys sent to get coal by their mother or father (who was probably downing the second or third pint in the Atlas). The bullyboys were always grubby, unshaven men with bad teeth, bad breath and a bad attitude.

When it was your turn to get coal, the 'merchant' would just stand and watch as a business CEO would. His henchmen would do the actual business.

"How much?" was the surly demand.

"Well, how much is it today?"

"A quid a hundredweight."

"Oh, that's a lot for coal."

"Do you want some or not?"

The coal buyer would then submit to the horrendous price in fear, desperation of being cold and the desire to be anywhere but there. In many cases, the older buyer would just get his or her bags filled—that was all they could carry.

If you were more fortunate, you would have borrowed a wheelbarrow to take home your load and thus save the struggle down Cattell Road to your house.

It was my turn next, and I had a nice big wheel barrow to take home my hundredweight (112 pounds). My load was quickly dumped into the barrow, the grubby helper bouncing the scales in his haste to get me gone and on to the next 'prey' and in doing so, giving me a lot less than my hundredweight. But when I reached home, how would I know or be able to prove so?

"Is he with you?" Mr. Grubby asked me.

I looked behind me and there was a little boy, no older than six or seven standing there in his under vest and short pants. The snow had been falling softly for about an hour, and the spot on his little bare shoulders where his braces were hanging was red with the cold. His nose was running; down the front of this face were two large, green 'candles,' he had no socks on and only old runners with holes in. His constant hacking cough from bronchitis was a sure sign of his condition, and a wondering of how he would get through the winter without proper food and clothing. Many times, the bronchitis in this damp, polluted air turned to pneumonia and an early demise of such souls as he.

He looked a sorry sight standing there looking like an ad for Oxfam in the flesh.

He was shuddering with the cold and his blue eyes looked up at Mr. Grubby with defiance and pride, "No, I'm by me-self!" he commented, "Fifty pounds, please." Mr. Grubby dumped the coal into the little tyke's cart which consisted of an orange box with a handle from a baby's pram set on an axel with two bicycle wheels. The whole contraption looked very unstable and weak, and I wondered how he would manage to make it home.

"Where's your dad?" I asked.

"Over in the pub," he motioned with his head toward the Atlas pub, holding on to the handle of his cart for dear life.

"How far do you have to go?" I asked.

"Down Garrison Lane to the flats," he replied.

I looked at my sturdy wheelbarrow and his frail cart. I had come to the coal yard complaining about my plight but now realised how fortunate I was.

The cold, wet little lad shuffled out of the yard and disappeared out of my sight as he went into Garrison Lane and his long, slow trudge to the flats; his feet now thoroughly wet from the melting snow, his heels showing though the back of his runners all red and swollen. When he arrived at his flats, there were no elevators to help him up to his flat; he would have to carry it up, one bucketful at a time, until the coalbunker was filled and his parents would expect a nice warm room from a crackling fire when they arrived home from their pub-crawling.

As years have gone by, I have often thought of this little lad and how and where he ended up. Did he get gobbled up by the local way of life, and perhaps become a coal man, or did he escape the web and break free to make a better life for himself in the world outside of Small Heath? Or is he now the current Mr. Grubby at the coal yard, struggling to stay ahead?

# 8. Johnny's Pup

The people in Cattell Road were ordinary working people who didn't have much but if you were in need they would share it with you. It was a case of paying it forward. One day they might need something and you could help. The kind of consideration that is short in supply in the modern world of today.

The houses in our part of the road were fronted right onto the sidewalk. That meant that as soon as you stepped out of the door, you stepped right onto the sidewalk—a stride's width from roadway where the city-bound vehicles rushed past on their missions to town, or out of it.

This included trams, buses, trucks and the ubiquitous cars of course.

It was a true main road and hazardous to the pedestrian who might need to cross over to the other side of the road. After a few years of practice, as a resident, you learned to cross by stepping with the traffic and pausing on the centreline for a break in the cars coming the other way. It was a skill developed by the indigenous over a long time. You learned to do this safely without any undue concern, but children were discouraged from doing this kamikaze routine until they were much older.

Our house had two steps down to the sidewalk, the houses on our side having been built higher from the ground than the houses across the other side of the road. This meant that the front doors of the houses opposite to us opened right onto the sidewalk—so you opened the door, stepped off the step and there you were standing on the sidewalk. In reality, a person in the houses opposite opened his front door and stepped right onto the sidewalk—often bumping into the person walking by.

My friend, by the name of Johnny, lived opposite us in such a house. He was my age, about ten years old.

He had no dad—didn't know where he was—a younger brother about 4 years old and a very tired mother who worked all hours she could to bring in enough money to pay the rent and buy food for the three of them.

Owing to the economic situation in the household, life was very Spartan; no extras, no treats and clothing looking like last year's left overs, but they were a happy family. The mother tried her best, loved them a lot and did the best she could.

Johnny knew this of his mom and so never complained. Sometimes, when he was over visiting and it was mealtime, Johnny would stay and eat with us. You could tell from the look in his eyes that what we considered normal was a feast and a treat for Johnny. My mother always used it as an example to make us realise just how lucky we were.

One day, Johnny came over to see us brimming over with excitement and grinning from ear to ear. In his arms he was clutching a little fuzzy puppy. He was so proud of his newfound friend that a brother of his mother had given him.

In reality, I think it was the very first pet that Johnny had ever owned.

Over the weeks, every time you saw Johnny, you saw the pup. Johnny never went anywhere without his little pal. He took it to bed, to the stores, even to the bathroom with him. Johnny and his little canine pal were inseparable. It was so nice to see Johnny happy with life and smiling instead of his perpetual worried frown from all the stresses he always bore as the older child, and the permanent babysitter for his little brother who could be very trying most of the time. It was so nice to see.

Johnny took his burden well and never complained, especially now he had his little pal.

Then one Saturday morning, came the most awful day in Johnny's life.

His mother had gone into work on overtime. She didn't want to go because that was when she did her shopping for the week and spent time with her family. Money was money, and in short supply in their house so in she had to go.

As usual, Cattell Road was very busy with all the cars, buses, trams, motorbikes—you name it, it was thundering along Cattell Road.

Then about 11 o'clock, there was this tremendous screaming of brakes and tires on the roadway as rubber bit into the blacktop of Cattell Road. The noise was so immense that everyone ran out onto the sidewalk to see what was going on—surely a nasty accident.

On the other side of the road, a double-decker corporation bus had stopped and the driver was out talking to someone on the other side of the bus. Being nosy, I crossed the road to see what was going on.

Johnny was sitting on the curb by the front wheel of the bus, screaming and crying like I have never seen anyone. As I came around the front of the bus I saw the reason for Johnny's distressed state.

Lying on the road, just behind the front tire of the bus was a mound of fur and blood and entrails, steaming in the cool Saturday morning air—hardly recognizable as Johnny's furry puppy just a few minutes before.

Johnny was out of his mind with grief. I have never seen anyone before or since in such a state, crying so hard I thought he would explode.

His whole world had just disappeared under the front wheel of a corporation bus.

His little brother had opened the front door to go out to play and left it ajar as he left. Puppies being like they are, had run out through the open door into oblivion—never to enjoy the cuddling and loving of the human to whom he had meant the whole world.

Nothing we said would console poor Johnny, he just cried and cried and cried. I didn't know what to do, or what to say—I just stood there and looked.

The poor bus driver tried to console him, but soon realised there was no way he could. He gave Johnny his bus number and name, and had to climb aboard to keep the bus schedule for his passengers.

The bus pulled away and there was Johnny, still sitting on the curb looking at the remains of his only love in life— the blood now starting to trickle into the gutter on its way to the drain.

Mr. Newey, who lived two doors down, appeared at the curb with a box of sawdust and a hearth shovel. He quietly covered the remains with the sawdust and gently lifted them into the cardboard box.

He silently handed Johnny the box and finished removing the remnants left behind in the gutter with his shovel.

Johnny just stood up, the box cradled in his arms and disappeared through the front door that had been the demise of his beloved.

In days to follow, I never knew how to broach the subject of his dead pal, and so as friends do, I just carried on as normal waiting for Johnny to mention it—but he never did.

# 9. Back Garden

The back yard was a rather unusual evolution of time. As you walked out of the kitchen into the yard, there was about four feet to the fence between us and the Smith family next door.

Turning left out of this back door (the other one, opposite on the other side of the kitchen led into the tunnel back entry. Once in the entry you could either turn left, down the entry into the road, or right, and end up in the back yard from another direction), and the blue brick yard led past the outdoor toilet (outdoor! It was the only toilet!), then the outhouse (where all the rubbish was stored).

At this point, there was a passageway on the blue bricks that ran parallel to the house across all of the houses just before the actual back garden.

Somewhere in the history of the houses, someone had decided that this 'common access' was unnecessary as the houses on either side of us had their own access through the entry.

For this reason, the three houses now had fences that ran from the back of the house to the bottom of the garden where the 'back houses' lay transversal to the direction of our houses. They gained access to their homes by going down the Smiths' entry.

As soon as you left the kitchen to go into the yard, you were faced with a high, wooden 'plank' fence that had obviously seen better days—it leaned very precariously in our direction but afforded us a narrow strip of garden along the fence line. That was, except for the area immediately opposite the back door. Here someone had concreted the area and this is where my mother kept her clothes wringer for use on washdays. At the end of the blue brick the true garden started. Well, if hard ground full of rocks and general pieces of metal bed frames and the like. At one time, someone had set a boundary between us and the Smiths by using the ingenuity of the local craftsman and using bedsteads, bedsprings and pieces of rusty sheet metal.

It all added to the ambience of the local area with its rust colour matching the cast-iron down-pipes of the houses.

Across the bottom of the garden, was a wooden picket fence that served to preserve the Pickering family's privacy in their yard of a few feet between their front door, and the pathway down to the Smiths' entry.

Running down the left of the garden, was a modern 'friendly neighbour' wooded fence that the Hathaway family Grandfather 'Bertie' had put up in his spare time. All in all, our garden was a sight to behold.

Our 'garden' had a pathway down the centre, with each side of the pathway lined with tilted house bricks to mark the boundary between the path and the garden. Why? I don't know, because the garden and the pathway looked the same!

After living with my Grandmother and Grandfather for so many years and enjoying a lovely flower garden, my heart ached for some flowers and a garden like I had been used to at my Grandparents.

To this end, I decided to ignore the rust and bedsprings and try to make it look more like a flower garden.

My parents weren't interested in gardening or looking after the back, so any 'agricultural' changes had to be made on my own effort and any money I could provide—which wasn't very much.

Not far up the road was a 'huxter' shop (a shop in the front room of someone's house. In those days, anyone could do it, there being no restriction or permit or licence) that catered to the local pigeon-flying fraternity. He sold corn, groats, wheat and anything else he could proffer to the pigeon fanciers.

In his shop, I had seen some gladiolus bulbs for sale and so took a walk up to see how much they were. He had obviously had them for some time and was more than willing to give me a deal. So, carrying my little bag of gladiolus corms, I returned home to plant my treasures.

Adjacent to the brick edge of the garden, was the path the clothesline took, with a post at each end of the garden. My mother would have to wipe it each time she used it to get rid of the grime and black that coated the line from the chimney smoke and the industrial pollution that was everywhere. To do this, she would walk along the top of the bricks at the edge of the garden as she was not tall enough to do it otherwise.

Not being the gardening type, she had no regard of empathy for those who did. This meant that my gladiola would be in jeopardy each time she hung out washing.

Something had to be done to keep the cats, next door's kids and my mother off my flowers.

I carefully dug the area where I was to plant the corms. I had no idea that fertiliser or even good soil was necessary to grow flowers. I had always followed around behind my Grandparents and they knew and did this without telling me. Anyway, the intent was there, and so in went my corms. To keep them safe, I found an orange box and split the wood off the pieces to make stakes and set the stakes in the ground above the corms to mark where they were.

All I could do now was wait. In those days, I didn't know that it is better to group glads; I set them out in two lines about two feet apart. I think I was expecting more floral output than glads give.

While waiting for my corms to show, there was something else I needed to do.

On a previous visit to my Grandparents, my Grandfather had given me a chicken so I could have fresh eggs. I named her 'Rosie' by which she was affectionately known until the day she died.

She didn't have a pen, but just roamed around the garden and slept in the outhouse at night. She never caused any trouble or asked for anything and was a good little chicken and occasionally gave us an egg or two.

Now with my flowers about to come out, I decided I had to make a pen so she wouldn't scratch up my flowers and destroy my garden.

How to make a chicken pen. Once again, money was not available and any pen had to come from my ingenuity and careful use of resources. I looked around and found just what I needed. A green table, about four feet by two. It had a top, a ledge about six inches off the ground and four legs. It was painted with glossy green paint which I knew would be waterproof. Next, I 'borrowed' a piece of the fence between us and the Smiths. It was the rails off a baby's cot that are normally lowered to get the child out. There were always house bricks about and I needed a few to complete my list of building materials.

So, I set the table up against the Pickering's fence at the bottom of the garden and closed in the open part of the table with pieces of wood everywhere except where I left a little door so she could come out. On the table ledge, I put a shallow cardboard box and put some grass and straw in it for her to lay her eggs in.

I now had to build a wall around her house with the house bricks I had found. I had long developed the skill of building little walls without mortar and content that the walls were safe and wouldn't fall on Rosie. In one of the walls, I put the crib rails as a gate and a place where I could look at her and she could look out at the rest of the world. She could put her neck out and look, but her body was too big to squeeze through the rails. This was Rosie's new house, or prison, depending on how you looked at it. She never complained, she never tried to fly over the top of the wall and gave me eggs until she died at a ripe old age.

Things were shaping up in my garden. Now to the next project—a house for my rabbit. I had used up all my resources building Rosie's pen, so there was nothing in the reserve in the outhouse to build a rabbit hutch.

Perseverance paid off. My mother told me she had been thinking about throwing out our sideboard because it was too big and bulky for the living room. So, out came the sideboard into the garden next to Rosie's chicken palace. I took out the doors and replaced them with chicken wire and voila, a rabbit pen. My garden was really looking up—a chicken pen, a rabbit hutch and a garden full of flowers— Wow! What more could a boy from Birmingham want?

When I was given the rabbit, I was told its name was Jack. Well, a short while later, Jack became Jacquie when lots of baby rabbits arrived one morning! What a surprise that was. My investment of one had become nine overnight. I now had to divide the rabbit hutch into separate quarters to house the growing family.

Next came the pigeon pen! My friend Len Pickering from over the back fence was very friendly with Tommy Newey who lived across the road and was the racing pigeon guru of the area. My father's family had always had racing pigeons and so at the mention of free racing pigeons, my father's ears pricked up and a pigeon pen was of the order.

My father had recently 'renovated' the front room with grain and stain decor, a result of which was that the old wooden Victorian shutters were taken down to become— wait for it—a pigeon pen. This took the place next to my flowers and across from Rosie. Because my father was very interested, nails, wood and all kinds of bits and pieces appeared to make way for the pigeons.

It turned out my father couldn't keep pigeons like his father had, and within a short time so many pigeons had died that Len took the remainder back to Tommy Newey and left the grand Victorian shutter pen to waste away to dereliction in my Garden of Eden.

When my flowers came up, I proudly cut the blossoms and took them inside to my mother—who didn't have time for anything or anyone, and couldn't have cared less or appreciated the effort I had put in to grow them.

After cutting glads, there isn't much left and so my garden became bare and sparse—not what I had dreamed of in my fantasies when I had been planting them. Once the flowers were gone, the rampant kids of next door and my brother's friends ruined what effort I had made by tramping the area, knocking down my sticks and my parents couldn't be bothered to appreciate what I had tried to do and told me not to make such fuss.

Ah, well, another time and another place.

# 10. Sitting on the Bus

Sitting on the bus, that's all my life seems to be. No, sitting in the classroom all day long with the master droning on about the philosophy of covalent compounds and tangents.

All I seemed to do in my life was bus ride to school, school, bus ride home, homework, go to bed, get up, ride to school...when does it end, or does it? I imagined myself going round and round and round for the foreseeable rest of my life.

When the bus from school arrived in Colmore Row, I had to walk to the other side of town to get the bus to my house. The normal was to walk via the churchyard of St. Phillips (Birmingham cathedral), its low walls now void of the beautiful iron railings seen in Victorian pictures.

They had been cut down with welding torches in the WWII drive for metal for warships and planes. Even before they were cut down, never to be replaced, the city fathers knew the actual metal value in the railings was unsuitable for the war effort but figured it showed a good example to the Birmingham people who would sacrifice their offerings.

The 'cathedral' was always a grey/black colour which I figured was caused by the smoke from industry in the Birmingham area. It turns out it was pigeon guano that was so thick, that when they removed it in the 1960s they found stone relief under it they never knew existed!

The culprits were everywhere in the churchyard, respondent to the many handouts from the local office workers who were always ready to share their lunches with them.

These feathered guano-makers were underfoot by the thousand. A sudden noise would cause a blackout of the sun as the huge flock took to the air momentarily. They were always quick to land again afraid of missing a morsel.

A road ran around the churchyard in what was referred to as a 'close.' In olden days, the gentry had occupied the beautiful Georgian and Victorian mansions that overlooked the cathedral.

These buildings were now the offices of prominent lawyers and doctors, still reflecting their pedigree architecture, wrought iron and polished front doors, complete with brass nameplates.

Birmingham is a hilly place and so it was that from the edge of the churchyard, the land ran in a quite steep hill down toward Corporation Street and the centre of the business district. To vary, I would take different routes.

One day I would take Cherry Street, trying to imagine where the cherry orchard had been. It was hard to dismiss all of the solid red brick and blacktop and imagine trees and verdant pastures!

At the bottom of the hill was Corporation Street. This was a very beautiful street architecturally with its cornices, pillars and marble facings. If I looked up to the second story, I could see even more grandeur in style that had disappeared from the street level. It turned out upon investigation that the location of Corporation Street had been the centre of one of Birmingham's worst slums, full of violence, disease, corruption and debauchery.

To combat this, the city fathers had literally driven a hole right through the middle of it, demolishing everything to right and left, and had built an 'avenue' of great design to imitate the Champs Elysée's in Paris, France. The idea was to open up the slums with high class building, lighting (still a new innovation), and 'up' the social level to improve the area by role modelling and expose the bad areas which the police would be easier to control beforehand; it was dangerous for even the 'peelers' to go in those areas.

It was like taking the lid off the sewer and seeing the rats scurry out of sight and leave the area. The move worked, but where did the rats go? Time had erased some of the glory and glamour on the street level as styles, time, and commerce had altered the storefronts to suit the current trends, but the upper stories still reflected the glitter of yesteryear.

As I crossed Corporation Street, I was at the top of Martineau Street (which, by the way, no longer exists). Martineau Street was another of the 'cut through and kill the slums' streets, named after a councillor of the times who had been instrumental in the slum clearance activities.

The street ran at an angle, which had always puzzled me. One day as I was walking down it to the High Street, I noticed a small opening in the buildings on my right. I walked over to it and to my pleasant surprise, saw it was a little lane about ten feet wide. It was so dark and dingy with its old, darkened bricks that it was understandable why I had not seen it before, it was more like a shadow than lane.

High up on the wall was a grimy sign that read 'Crooked Lane.' It certainly was, and lived up to its name admirably.

As narrow as it was, it twisted and turned quite a few times as it progressed down the hill parallel to Martineau Street.

On the one side of it was a high, brick wall that backed a huge building on Corporation Street. On the other side, to my surprise were some 'right out of Dickens' stores, still with their old-fashioned lamps hanging outside their doors, complete with leaded-light windows and wooden boards announcing the storekeepers' wares and names.

A strange phenomenon of Crooked Lane was its very steep and high curbs. The roadway itself was still in cobblestones, the only place I had ever seen this in Birmingham—except that is for the old bullring.

It was like walking through a time capsule. Sadly, none of the stores seemed currently in business. The new 'Parisienne' glamour of Martineau and Corporation Streets had obviously claimed their business with glittering new storefronts, but it was so nice to get a glimpse of the way life used to be and was still there for those who wanted to see how it was.

Today, I still think of that walk down Crooked Lane and how I could easily have never seen the Birmingham of yesteryear if I hadn't taken a slight detour. I now came out of the bottom of Crooked Lane into the bottom of Martineau Street.

As all the streets behind me were sloping downwards toward where the River Rea had been, this juncture of Martineau Street was also the juncture of Bull Street which approached from the left.

Bull Street had been famous for its butchers and meat shops. In the old days, the butchers would hang their sides of beef and the like outside the front of their stores for all to see without having to advertise.

Bull Street had been rebuilt many times as the huge weights of the carcasses had damaged the building fronts of the old Tudor-style timbered buildings.

When I crossed High Street on my way to Carrs Lane to catch my bus home, something make me walk across to the top of Albert Street opposite instead of turning right. Albert Street had been another 'cut through the slums' project in Queen Victoria's time. I glanced down Albert Street, and imagine my surprise when I noticed just inside Albert Street another 'shadow' like I had seen at the top of Martineau Street.

I hurried across to investigate, using the men's Victorian-style urinal in the centre of the High Street as a traffic refuge, and imagine how surprised and thrilled I was to see a sign on the wall that read, 'Crooked Lane!'

This Crooked Lane wound down the side and parallel to Albert Street in the same way as the one I had just discovered off Martineau Street. The same curbs, stores, lights, windows everything the same!

It was then that I realised, that both the parts of Crooked Lane had at one time been one lane that had wound its way up the hill from the bottom of Albert Street all the way to the former cherry orchards of Cherry Street!

It was just the interceding streets had cut it up into pieces, step by step, until that all that was left was the two pieces I had found surviving in spite of development and 'progress.'

As this had been a rural area (the orchards proved this), I began to think about what it must have been like when Crooked Lane was a narrow lane snaking its way up the hillside because of the hills steepness (as well as springs which were prominent in the area).

This was probably a well-used route and hence the development of stores along it route. The steep curbs were probably a defence against the water running down the hill, taking it away from the doorways of the businesses.

Having made this discovery, I was quite chuffed and hurried to catch my bus in Carrs Lane, just a block away.

I was soon sitting again, this time waiting for the circuitous routed bus to take me the three miles to Small Heath, and home. I jumped off the bus, full of my discovery and wanting to tell someone who cared. When my parents arrived home I was so full of excitement to share with them the finds I had made.

Guess what? They weren't interested.

Sometime later, I shared my discovery with my Grandfather Horton. He remembered Crooked Lane as a young boy, it being a lot more complete in those days. He had lived not far away from the area and so could fill me in on details that just nagged at me. In fact, in later years, he had 'fire watched' in WWII in this area and told me of damage to the area that had resulted in removal of other parts of Crooked Lane.

Ah, well, time for homework, time for bed—and then back to the routine—sitting, sitting and sitting.

# 11. Observations of a Boy From Birmingham

Just for something to do differently, I decided to sit on the front step of our house in Cattell Road, Small Heath, Birmingham, and just watch the people going by to see what people do when they don't know you're watching them.

The houses around where we lived had been built in about 1875 in an attempt to provide housing for the great migration to Birmingham by the rural dwellers who came to Birmingham to make their fortunes in the factories of the industrial revolution.

This was now 1958, so as you can imagine, the houses—including ours—were showing a little worse for wear.

To give the Victorian builders their due, they certainly knew how to build houses that were meant to last. The very typical red brick of the era was ubiquitous and left no doubt as to when and who had built them.

Nevertheless, even Victorian buildings will start to groan and complain a little after eighty-three years. The bricks on the outside of the house were looking a little worse for the ages of smoke, smog, acid rain and general pollution.

Their honeycomb appearance made me think that if that is what the ambient weather had done to the bricks, what price my lungs!

The front door was your typically a four-panel solid door with a huge square, iron lock bolted to the door on the inside. Its old-fashioned large key would grind in the lock the few times that anyone came to the front door instead of the side door in the entry.

The house had one time been a shop, known locally as an 'uxter' shop. In the days before permits and licences, anyone could open a shop in the front room of the house. This was original free enterprise, encouraged in the early days of the industrial revolution to add to the growing economy of the town.

As a result of the obvious many years the house had been a 'front room' shop, the solid concrete bottom step of the two steps to the front door showed its submission to the foot traffic of hob-nailed boots by the severe depression in the top surface.

Knowing how tough old concrete is, I wondered just how many customers it had taken to take such a toll.

Next to the front door was a bay window; two panes in the front, one on each side. This, too, was showing its age. The complete bay window was hung on the face of the building. After eighty-three years, it was still hanging— just.

From the inside of the room, looking out, it was good advice not to lean too far out to look through the windows and never to put your weight on the window by resting a foot on the shelf that was the bottom of the bay window. In fact, it was quite concerning to be looking out of the window and to be able to see the sidewalk through cracks in the joints of the window.

When a bus went by—well the dust that came through the cracks was alarming. When we had moved into the house, the huge, wooded Victorian shutters were still there. The weight alone of the shutters threatened to collapse the bay window into the street and so my father removed them to give further life to the already suffering structure.

I sat on the top step, wondering what type of shop it had been and what kind of display would have been in the window. A glance up the road to the left showed other dinosaurs from the front room store era.

On the corner of Arsenal Street, opposite the Marquis of Lorne pub was such a relic. It still had the square, steel tobacco ad panels attached to the front of the building below the store windows.

A permanent 'closed' sign on the door hinted of previous business when tobacco and smoking were vogue. The images on the glossy panels had badly oxidised, and patches of rust were now showing all over them, making for a very drab appearance to the building and the corner of the road. It had probably been a newsagent; common in that area at one time.

Its place in commerce had been taken by a similar, newer venture operated by Mr. and Mrs. Burke just two doors down from the corner.

My friend lived in the house in between these two entrepreneurial ventures. His house front was like the abandoned one on the corner, except the panels had been removed and sheets of plywood were now in place, giving the front a totally dead, abandoned look. As you might imagine, from the corner down didn't give a very good impression of the success of the road.

Stores like these two abandoned businesses dotted the sides of Cattell Road all the way from the Atlas Pub to the Greenway Pub, at the junction of Cattell Road and Coventry Road. It made me wonder if Cattell Road had once been a thriving Victorian metropolis of front-room huxter shops, now forgotten in the advance of time and progress, or whether the participants had been would-be business people who didn't recognise that huxter stores didn't work in Cattell Road and just joined the line of failed, failing and soon-to-be failing ventures.

Sometimes the dogged spirit of Brummies (citizen of Birmingham), never-to-give-up attitude can also be a definite disadvantage when you risk the family fortune on a hope and personal conviction that you will succeed where the rest of the road has failed.

Sometimes in life we are moving so fast, even though we are not aware of it, that we don't stop to truly see the life and living around us. Sitting on the top step, watching the road life was a very interesting exercise. So much happens that is 'normal,' that we don't stop to ask why or when or what.

Up to about 1950, Cattell Road had proffered a tram service. The lines ran down the centre of the road. When this service was first introduced in the late 1800s, it was probably a huge success for the Birmingham city football ground at the lower end of Cattell Road. Instead of having to navigate the hilly area with horses, the 'Blues' supporter could just hop a tram and be there in record time.

Come to think of it, that was probably the reason for half of the little shops in Cattell Road—preying on the football crowd before and after the game. The convenience trade most probably died a natural death with the coming of the omnibus that was even faster (the first ones were steam driven).

These originated in the city centre, and the fans probably picked up their treats there at much lower prices than the Cattell Road traders.

I noticed that there were always children moving along the road. Children, children, children. Where did they all come from? Most of them I didn't recognise as locals. They were always moving along the sidewalk with a distant look in their eyes.

Always looking way down the road. What was their mission in life that they didn't have time to be normal—like kicking a can along the sidewalk—annoying, but kid-like. How about skipping along with a song and a smile? What happened to the mischievous little tyke that used to ring the bell and run away?

I watched the puerile population very carefully, until one day I realised that most of these children didn't have both parents, or even if they did, they were never home. The children had forsaken their youthful pursuits to take responsibility of life—theirs, and usually younger siblings.

There was no time to be a kid and do kid things that could be remembered in the later years of life as fun. These children were very streetwise. There was nothing you could put over them—survivalists to the nth degree.

Mostly, they concentrated on finding sufficient food. There were no frills to life—no candy, ice cream, cakes—

just hard graft; getting home from school, making a fire, sweeping the house, getting as much of the evening meal ready as they could.

Then there was the dusting, the vacuuming and always homework from school. There was no exemption from any of the chores regardless of how much homework there was afterwards.

If the younger siblings were slack, as most of them were, the older one had to make up extra for the slider. The parent didn't care who did what, just that it had better be done.

So, with life like this, what was there to smile about as you wended your weary way to work? To children like this, childhood was cleaning, polishing, sweeping, errands and chores—no impression or thought of play and friends—when were you supposed to do that? There was never any time.

To add grist to the mill, after a hard day being a kid in these conditions, the parent often rewarded the effort with complaints about things that weren't to the satisfaction of the task giver, never a compliment for the things done—tomorrow was another day, and another day of effort that went unheeded.

Little old ladies were in plentiful supply in Cattell Road. I don't know what happened to the little old men, but there were old ladies to spare! They were always walking up and down, up and down, up and down.

Where they went and where they came from, no one seemed to know, but they did an awful lot of it and each and every day. Was it the bookie's shop? Was it a sly glass of Guinness at the Marquis? Was it a place where little old ladies found a supply of little old men who would listen to their woes and wishes?

Who knows, but it was a full-time occupation—whatever they were doing. Surprisingly, few had canes or walkers as seen today. Some were slower than others, but many were spry and springy in their step—maybe it was little old men!

Cattell Road was in the middle of what is now nicely called 'socially economically depressed'—a fancy word for poor, out-of-work, unskilled, no-chance-of-job etc. etc. etc. Owing to this, a common sight was pregnancy. Not happy, 'oh, how lovely, we're having a little one,' but more like, 'here we go again, another kid!' It was almost like a booby prize at a fair—you took a chance and every game a winner! Women of thirty years of age looked haggard and old; depressed, wrinkled, dishevelled hair, no makeup, no smile and dressed in clothes that even the thrift store would refuse.

This was an accepted way of life. No hope, no money, no job—just a dreary existence of day after day poverty, rewarded on Saturday by another day of poverty. Often they were the third or fourth generation of this thinking.

Quite often, drinking contributed to this state of despair and so the syndrome continued to the next generation. In many cases, the worn-out wives would take in washing or ironing to help the meagre income. Such effort, for so little pittance, would contribute to the helpless feeling of non-achievement in their lives.

There was no beginning, there was no end—it just went on and on as it had always since they were young. Their parents had lived this life, as had their parents, so what was wrong—this was the model they were following. If a person tried to get out of the mould, the lack of confidence, clothing, fear of rejection by peers if they tried to better themselves and general lack of ability just kept them in the gutter. Most had no initiative to want to better themselves.

Or rather, they had become so old on life and beaten down by the time they were twelve years old, that there was no desire or energy to get up and out. Besides, once any of these children opened their mouths it was pretty obvious where they came from. As soon as they opened their mouth, the phonetics said 'working class' or 'poorly educated' or 'brown collar, not suitable consideration for anything other than working in the factory.'

When Marie Antoinette said, "Let them eat cake if they have no bread," she hadn't been to Birmingham; they didn't have cake—and very little bread!

Unless you have been there and tasted the true meaning of life in the rough, or better, no life in the rough, hearsay news of an area on national news is just a collection of adjectives, adverbs and descriptive epithets.

The number 54 bus ran down Cattell Road. Its route was from Stechford to Carrs Lane in the city centre, where I caught the bus to go home. The buses were cream and dark blue, the colours of the Birmingham City Motor Corporation.

The earlier ones were real boneshakers, and the ride from town was anything but smooth. However, when the corporation brought out the new Daimler buses—well that was a cool ride. The best ride was upstairs, sitting over the top of the driver. Also, you had a good view of everything.

The worst was at the back on the three-seater, in front of the emergency exit window at the back of the upstairs deck. My friend showed me one day just how easily the window opened, and I often wondered if you would get trampled in the crush if it was ever needed to be used in an emergency.

At one time, my mother worked at the Coventry Road bus depot cleaning the buses. The cleaners stood on scaffold that ran alongside the buses and cleaned them by hand. My mother didn't like climbing the scaffold, and rather than climb down and then back up she preferred to climb on to the top of the bus while the other workers moved the scaffold around the bus to the other side and then climb back on to the scaffold. The foreman thought she was crazy!

The bus drivers drove their buses like one of the four men of the apocalypse—crazy, but accurate. How they manipulated those big buses around the small, tight corners, I will never know.

One day though, when the council workmen were tearing up the tramlines in the middle of Cattell Road, one bus driver tried to cut it a little too fine in his judgement of the distance of the roadwork to the curb.

I was sitting on the step watching the workmen, always a good pastime for kids, when the bus's front curb side wheel mounted the sidewalk and the side of the bus hit the cast-iron light pole standard that was just to the side of our front door.

There was a tremendous bang as the bus caught the pole and the glass in the window next to the pole shattered and a huge piece of it fell in to the bus.

Unfortunately, a woman had been sitting there and caught the full weight and force of the broken pane. Safety glass is designed to shatter into small pieces, so after the initial wallop onto the top of her head, she was then showered with hundreds of shards of broken window.

The bus came to an immediate stop, still up the curb, and the bus driver jumped out of his cab and ran around to see what had happened. Well, there was chaos, screaming, crying and oh, lots of blood—lots and lots of blood!

The bus conductor took charge and broke out the first aid kit and tried to assist the shocked lady who minutes before had been quietly reading her book. The ambulance was quickly there, and the lady taken away to the hospital. The bus could not be moved until the police arrived and investigated, so now besides the roadwork causing congestion, the bus had plugged up the one side of the road completely.

Goodness knows what the driver had to explain, I felt kind of sorry for him. The other passengers were moved to a replacement bus and the damaged one was eventually taken away to the garage.

With that excitement over, I settled down to watch the workmen getting these embedded tramlines out of the black top in the road. They were using pneumatic jackhammers to get down under the lines so that they could be prized up and taken away in sections.

The compressor used to power these hammers made an awful racket, and the operators didn't think of using earplugs. The jackhammer operators were always burly laborers, mostly Irish, with huge muscles from wrestling these iron monsters, and they always seemed to have big bellies which they rested on top of the jackhammer handles.

I never quite knew if this was just a place to rest their beer bellies, or the corpulence was actually a way of balancing the jackhammer and levering it where they wanted it to go.

The jack hammering was hot and dirty work. The workers had to stop occasionally to get a drink, to stop the tremendous dehydration they must have been suffering.

All workmen crews came with a brazier. What is a brazier? It's a metal bin, rather like a small oil drum, that has holes punched in the side and is usually on three legs. The workmen fill it with coke and fire it up with a device that looks like a small flamethrower. The 'flame thrower' is actually used to soften the blacktop when they are doing surface repairs on the road, but for most times it's used for starting the brazier so they can boil water for tea.

The workmen's tea break is a part of work lore—totally sacred and never challenged, even by the foreman. Each workman has a billycan that consists of a can, about a litre in size, which has a top that serves also as a cup and a heavy wire handle by which the workman carries his can.

The can is usually dark blue enamel, and each workman puts his water in his can and sits it on top of the grid that sits on top of the brazier. When the water boils, a spoonful of tea, sugar and milk is added to the can—the cup top is jammed into place—and then the can is swung around and around the workman's head until he figures it's mixed enough.

This done, the cup top is removed, filled with tea and supped like ambrosia. What about the tea leaves? What tea leaves? The contents are consumed with pleasure and contentment incomparable to anything in the world—and then back to work.

At night, a night watchman would keep the work area safe. He was normally a retired senior who didn't mind doing the boring, often cold, job of watching the work area for pilferers and vandals.

He would sit in his hut; a small, portable hut just big enough to shelter him from the elements, and usually stare at the bright coke brazier while he drank his tea, ate his sandwiches and read yesterday's newspaper.

It was a lonely job, no one would ever speak to him, and of course his job meant he was working from 7 pm to 7 am. Occasionally, if the work area was more than he could see from his chair or stool, he would get up and walk around to check things, often out of boredom and for something to do.

Tar pots that flamed this way and that into the dark reaches of the night usually lit up the work area. If one of the tar pots ran out of tar, or the wind blew it out, the watchman would relight it—often the most exciting thing of his night. If anyone came near, he was usually sent on his way with a gruff rebuttal and a gesture—it was no place for a social interaction that was for sure.

When morning came, the night watchman would dissolve from view to wherever watchmen go in the daytime (probably underground) and reappear like magic the next night. I often wondered where the city found these thespians of the night.

Was there a night watchman's union, or maybe a brotherhood of night purveyors? Wherever they came from, they were usually older, usually portly gentlemen; unshaven, poorly but warmly dressed and scared little boys to death!

Another notability of the local populace was the state of dress—or lack of it. In the nineteenth century before the industrial revolution, many people worked as servants, gardeners etc. at the big mansion houses in the still rural areas of Warwickshire. I had often wondered what it was that made a maid instantly identifiable as a maid, when to me the styles of dress looked all the same.

It turns out, that in order to identify the 'service' staff and to make sure they remained feeling servile, the people 'in service' were always dressed in the previous generation's clothing style.

Well, in Cattell Road, there were no in-service maids or assistance workers, but they were definitely dressed in the previous generation's style of clothing. However, this was not a class distinction; they were just still wearing it from the previous generation because they didn't have anything else and were probably wearing their family's hand-me-downs from way back.

It was most noticeable in the footwear, especially among the children. Shoes were ill-fitting, scruffy (never seen the polish tin), backs broken down, laces broken or missing, often with holes in them.

One little boy I saw was obviously wearing a woman's pair of high-heel shoes that had had the heels cut off level to make them level as boys' shoes are. He was too poor to be proud or even aware of the social statement he was making—he was just happy to have some shoes, many went around in holey runners or even worse, nothing at all.

Washday was an exercise in futile progression. The idea of washing clothes is to have clean clothes the next day. Getting them is a wonder of human initiative. In Small

Heath, there were no domestic washing machines, drying machines; just the copper in the back kitchen where the water was boiled.

Usually coal fired, later gas fired. When this water had boiled, the person doing the washing had to bale it into a large, metal tub, usually positioned in the yard by the mangle or wringer. The hot was mixed with cold until the temperature was just right.

Next, either washing powder, or old soap bits in a perforated container, was introduced to the tub and shaken about to get the soapy foam going in the tub. The dirty clothes were dumped into the tub and agitated up and down in the soapy water by a 'squasher.'

This was a bell-shaped metal device full of holes on a long pole handle. The contents were squashed up and until the washer decided the dirt had all been loosened from the clothes. This done, the clothes were removed from the tub and wrung by hand to get the majority of the water out and then put in a washing basket. The dirty water from the tub was tipped into the yard and allowed to run down the closest drain.

Now it was time to rinse.

The tub was refilled with cold water, and the 'squashing' began all over again. Depending on the dirtiness and soapiness of the load, this rinsing was done once or twice until all the soap had been removed. The clothes were then again wrung out as much as possible by hand and placed yet again in the basket.

Now, it was time to wring all of the excess water out of the clothes in preparation to putting them on the clothesline to dry.

The good old-fashioned wringer, or mangle as some called it, did this job very well. The wringer consisted of two rollers made of wood, that were attached to each other at each end, by iron gears attached to a big wheel with a wooden handle on it.

The rollers could be adjusted by a control handle above the iron gears. As the gears were iron, they had to be kept greased to prevent their rusting. This ubiquitous gear oil had a bad habit of getting connected to the nice clean, white washing, especially the sheets as they were so wide and took up so much of the rollers.

The washing was introduced to the rollers, and the big wheel at the end of the rollers turned to force the washing through the rollers. The water squeezed out would run out of a hole at the front of the wringer into the tub from which the washing had come.

Sometimes, catching the washing as it came out of the back of the wringer was an acquired art to prevent its doubling round onto the oily gears.

So now you had a basket full of clean, wringed washing. Time to go on the line. The washing lines were suspended between two posts, one at each end of the garden. The lines were left out all the time, so the first thing that had to be done was to run a wet cloth along the line to remove the black gunk that had settled on it from the previous night.

Once dusk came, as darkness descended, so did the airborne dirt, smog and pollution. If you had dared to put your washing on the line without wiping it, the whole lot would have had a black line on it where it touched the line.

Sometimes, when the line was full and the prop pushed under the middle of the line to give it height for better drying, the strain would prove to be too much and the line would break, dumping the washing onto the muddy garden—another round of rinsing and wringing!

And better not forget to get it in before the dusk arrives!

Some of the houses built in the back area of the main houses, usually on self-sufficient yards, had to take turns using the washing facilities. If you missed your day, or dropped it in the mud—too bad, have to wait until next week.

Water was plentiful in Birmingham from the Elan Valley in Wales—beautiful, soft water. It seems, though, that many of the local indigenous had never heard of a tap, or worse, a flannel and soap.

There seemed to be no shame in this. True, in Victorian times, it was considered weakening to wash too often; once or twice a year was considered adequate. Well, the pedestrian traffic along our road were certainly taking this to heart. They should have been very strong by the looks of things—and smelly!

Deodorant was considered unnatural, washing was weakening; there seems to be an oxymoron syndrome somewhere here!

As Birmingham was at the centre of Mercia—an original Saxon stronghold where at a time in history, the warring overlords decided to call it quits—it meant that there was a mixing of races at the centre of the Birmingham area. If you look at the political map of Birmingham today, the districts radiate out from the centre of old Birmingham, roughly the Digbeth/Deritend area.

The Old Crown pub in Deritend is probably the true centre of 'Bermicham,' 'Brummagem,' 'Brum' or 'Birmingham.'

Even in the Saxon days, Birmingham was a melting pot; its Creole dialect made up of Roman, German, French, Celtic (Welsh, Cornish, Cumbrian), Angle and Saxon, must make it the biggest mix of dialects in Britain. No wonder visitors had a hard time understanding the gathering dialect of the industrial revolution clans.

Sometimes, they even have a hard time understanding each other!

It is a hard-sounding dialect, having evolved as a nasal dialect; possibly because of the respiratory problems the Brummies encountered as a result of the industrial outfall of smoke, coal gas, smog and general pollution.

Although this was greatly improved in the 1960–70s with the Clean Air Act, the dialect was by then totally embedded in the local folklore and became a learned thing. New arrivals in the Birmingham area found it 'cool' to speak this way as a sign of the 'in' crowd, and a way of seeking acceptance of their new arrival in the area and avoiding being identified as an outsider if you sounded like Hagrid from Harry Potter.

The dialect was further modified with the arrival of the new immigrants from Asia and East India in the 1960s. The plentiful supply of jobs and comparative wealth attracted many newcomers to the area.

This modified the area demographically and racially as in the time of Hengist and Horsa, in the dark ages after the Romans and prior to the Norman invasion.

The English language is a Creole language made up of the races mentioned earlier. The emergence of Britain as a world power guaranteed that the language would never sit still, its content constantly being added to as each country and population was introduced to the British way of life.

The servicemen and politicians brought many new words to the table and in the fashion of the time, showed their 'education' by bringing new words to court. Queen Victoria loved these additions from her 'people,' almost as much as she loved her Prince Albert.

Small Heath was doing today what it had done for generations—it was living. It was a living, thriving, moving, happening place where the comings and goings of its mosaic of people added their bit to the puzzle and then went on their way.

They had no notion of the part they were playing in the evolution of Brummies, Birmingham or the future of the area that continually moved toward a newer time.

Cattell Road was, as Shakespeare said, a stage, and all the locals of Cattell Road were players on it. The only difference was this play had no end—it just kept playing for the benefit of mankind.

# 12. The Blocks in the Road

I was walking home from school in Small Heath, Birmingham, in the heart of England. Happy to be on my way home from Saint Benedict's school on the hill above Saint Benedict's Church, which sat on the corner of Saint Benedict's Road and Coventry Road.

I was getting very wet! The rain was just driving it down. The rainfall was so heavy it was hard to even see across the road, and it had been like that for over an hour. Where did all this rain come from? I had to run all the way home from school in this torrent and it didn't look like stopping. I was soaked to the skin.

Well, I had left the school and as there was no one there to meet me and it was raining so hard, I had decided to run down the hill to Coventry Road, turn right and run like heck to my house just along the road at 728.

On the way up the road, I had noticed that the road had started to lift in a few places. I couldn't quite understand how a road could lift and leave holes and some of them big ones, right where the traffic was driving.

I looked again and saw that for some reason, it was in the gutter that this was mainly happening.

Standing now, in the shelter of the overhang of the front door. I stood and watched. These old Victorian houses had some good points and this was one of them; the wide, masonry overhangs built to protect the front door from the weather.

The gutter was completely awash with torrents of water heading for the drains, but it seemed the drains couldn't cope with the deluge and so there was a backup of water in the gutters making it look like a river.

I looked carefully to see this lifting and it was then I noticed that when a vehicle came too close to the curb, the front wheel would seem to go down a hole as the car dipped a little.

When the buses came by, this situation was magnified by the huge wheels of the corporation bus. As the buses passed, they would push the water to the side. It was then that I saw what was happening.

For some reason, the gutter roadway seemed to be made of tarred, wooden blocks that had been tamped in under extreme pressure. Why wood? I couldn't for the life of me see why—but there they were.

A few more buses went by, and each time one did, I saw a block thrown up by the back tire of the bus's curb wheel. Eventually, this consistent treatment of the road was developing quite a sizeable hole in the roadway.

There were so many blocks free now, that they were starting to float down the gutter on the back of the torrent—headed for who knows where.

I knew that the price of coal was quite high at the time, and my parents had a hard time making ends meet. So, with this in mind, I was determined not to let a combustible, well-tarred, roadblock go to waste.

Wet is wet, so standing in the doorway soaked to the skin I could hardly get any wetter. So, I ran down the steps, along the path, through the gateway and over to the curb. A quick look right and left—it was too rainy and dark for anyone to see what I was about to do—I grabbed one of these blocks and ran like mad for the front door of the house.

Making it up to the kitchen (we lived in the upstairs flat), I proudly presented my prize to my mother. She immediately saw the economic advantage of my acquisition, ignored my wet state and proceeded to make kindling for the fire.

Just in case it was a long night, I retraced my steps for block number two. It was easier the second time, and I was just at the top of the front steps, almost safe, when I paused and looked back to the scene of my crime.

Horrors! The 'man' (as anyone in authority was called) from the estates was walking along the curb collecting the loose blocks and piling them on the curb next to the hole.

He looked a little puzzled and was looking in the direction of the water flow in the gutter. He was trying to work out how he could have lost two blocks so soon, after responding to the report someone had phoned in about loose blocks in the roadway.

He looked up, then down the road. Finally, he shrugged his shoulders and walked off just as the 'workmen' arrived to repair the hole with the rescued blocks.

I always wondered what they did about the missing blocks—but for now, I was upstairs to the kitchen to keep warm on this nasty night and enjoy the spoils of my crime!

# 13. The Moneybox

In the late 1940s, Birmingham, England, was still recovering from the scars and damage of the war. Everywhere in the city centre, there was evidence of the nightly bombings from Germany during the blitz years.

The German air force had mistakenly deduced that as Birmingham was an industrial city, its war-making machine would be in or near the centre, just like Manchester, London or Coventry.

Just because the aerial photographs the Luftwaffe took of Birmingham during the day didn't show factories, was taken as the fact that must still be there but were camouflaged. So, night after night the centre of the city would be bombed.

What the Germans had missed, was the facts that Birmingham's munitions factories were spread around the outskirts of the town, not in the middle of it!

The Birmingham bullring was a bombers landmark and used as a reference for locating the bomb targets. Subsequently, when the German bombers were under pressure to bomb and run, they often just dumped their bomb load and ran, under the intense anti-aircraft fire from the gun batteries.

The poor old bullring had been there since beginning of time and had acquired its name because of bull baiting in the market place. As Birmingham was a hilly place, the bullring was on the side of a hill.

At the top of the hill was the 'new' street, the beginning of the newer part of the medieval town, and on the bottom of the hill was St Martin's Church. In between the two, on the 'hillside' was the mixture of stores that had evolved over the time of the city's early industrial revolution development.

Hence to say there was little if no planning, just stores here and there.

One of these on the mid hillside was the old market hall, on the left as you looked up the hill. It had grown from a collection of shanty shacks with dubious construction techniques, to a raised market with a beautiful flight of stone steps leading up to this showcase of commercial enterprise. A beautifully designed glass-domed roof crowned this.

That is until the night of August 25, 1944, when a well-aimed German bomb went right through the glass roof and destroyed the market along with a very expensive clock that had been moved there from the Imperial Arcade in Dale End in 1936 by the city fathers for 'safety.' The clock had originally been made by W. Potts of Leeds in 1883.

Actually, there were two bombs; as it was customary for bombers carrying such bombs to have. The first one destroyed the market hall and the second…

Well, it hit the centre of the bullring and…just lay there! When the bomb disposal experts came to defuse it, they found that the firing pin had been hammered down to make it useless and not explode, and alongside it was a note with the words 'Good luck, from the Czechs!'

The 500-pound egg shaped bomb had been made in one of the forced labour camps in Czechoslovakia, and the forced workers, at risk to themselves, had immobilised the bomb to save the poor English at least one lot of bomb damage.

The bomb was such an example of human kindness that the Birmingham City Council decided to use it for another kind of humane act.

After the war, this very same bomb was to be found resting inside the market hall (still roofless, but with makeshift stores all around the original market area) but this time on a stand.

It had been made into a moneybox for the orphaned children of the war.

My father took me there one day and gave me a sixpence which I was asked to place in the slot in the moneybox for the children less fortunate than I was.

This was a good example to me as a small child, how a bad thing can sometimes be made into a good thing.

I wonder if it's still there.

# 14. Washday

Washday was an exercise in futile progression. The idea of washing clothes is to have clean clothes the next day. Getting them is a wonder of human initiative. In Small Heath, there were no domestic washing machines, drying machines, just the copper in the back kitchen where the water was boiled.

Usually coal fired, later gas fired. When this water had boiled, the person doing the washing had to bale it into a large, metal tub, usually positioned in the yard by the mangle or wringer.

The hot was mixed with cold until the temperature was just right. Next, either washing powder, or old soap bits in a perforated container was introduced to the tub and shaken about to get the soapy foam going in the tub.

The dirty clothes were dumped into the tub and agitated up and down in the soapy water by a 'squasher.' This was a bell-shaped metal device full of holes on a long pole handle. The contents were squashed up and until the washer decided the dirt had all been loosened from the clothes.

This done, the clothes were removed from the tub and wrung by hand to get the majority of the water out and then put in a washing basket. The dirty water from the tub was tipped into the yard and allowed to run down the closest drain.

Now it was time to rinse. The tub was refilled with cold water, and the 'squashing' began all over again. Depending on the dirtiness and soapiness of the load, this rinsing was done once or twice until all the soap had been removed. The clothes were then again wrung out as much as possible by hand and placed yet again in the basket.

Now it was time to wring all of the excess water out of the clothes in preparation to putting them on the clothesline to dry.

The good old-fashioned wringer, or mangle as some called it, did this job very well. The wringer consisted of two rollers made of wood, that were attached to each other at each end by iron gears attached to a big wheel with a wooden handle on it.

The rollers could be adjusted by a control handle above the iron gears. As the gears were iron, they had to be kept greased to prevent their rusting. This ubiquitous gear oil had a bad habit of getting connected to the nice clean, white washing, especially the sheets as they were so wide and took up so much of the rollers.

The washing was introduced to the rollers and the big wheel at the end of the rollers turned to force the washing through the rollers. The water squeezed out would run out of a hole at the front of the wringer into the tub from which the washing had come. Sometimes, catching the washing as it came out of the back of the wringer was an acquired art to prevent its doubling round onto the oily gears.

So now you had a basket full of clean, wringed washing.

Time to go on the line. The washing lines were suspended between two posts, one at each end of the garden. The lines were left out all the time, so the first thing that had to be done was to run a wet cloth along the line to remove the black gunk that had settled on it from the previous night.

Once dusk came, as darkness descended, so did the airborne dirt, smog and pollution. If you had dared to put your washing on the line without wiping it, the whole lot would have had a black line on it where it touched the line.

Sometimes when the line was full and the prop pushed under the middle of the line to give it height for better drying, the strain would prove to be too much and the line would break, dumping the washing onto the muddy garden—another round of rinsing and wringing!

And better not forget to get it in before the dusk arrives!

Some of the houses built in the back area of the main houses, usually on self-sufficient yards, had to take turns using the washing facilities. If you missed your day, or dropped it in the mud too bad, have to wait until next week.

# 15. Tramlines

When it was time to take up the tramlines in Cattell Road, I settled down to watch the workmen getting these embedded tramlines out of the black top in the road. They were using pneumatic jackhammers to get down under the lines so that they could be prized up and taken away in sections.

The compressor used to power these hammers made an awful racket—and the operators didn't think of using earplugs. The jackhammer operators were always burly laborers, mostly Irish, with huge muscles from wrestling these iron monsters, and they always seemed to have big bellies which they rested on top of the jackhammer handles.

I never quite knew if this was just a place to rest their beer bellies, or the corpulence was actually a way of balancing the jackhammer and levering it where they wanted it to go.

The jack hammering was hot and dirty work. The workers had to stop occasionally to get a drink to stop the tremendous dehydration they must have been suffering.

All workmen crews came with a brazier. What is a brazier? It's a metal bin, rather like a small oil drum that has holes punched in the side and is usually on three legs. The workmen fill it with coke and fire it up with a device that looks like a small flamethrower. The 'flame thrower' is actually used to soften the blacktop when they are doing surface repairs on the road, but for most times it's used for starting the brazier so they can boil water for tea.

The workmen's tea break is a part of work lore—totally sacred and never challenged, even by the foreman. Each workman has a billycan that consists of a can, about a litre in size, which has a top that serves also as a cup, and a heavy wire handle by which the workman carries his can.

The can is usually dark blue enamel and each workman puts his water in his can and sits it on top of the grid that sits on top of the brazier. When the water boils, a spoonful of tea, sugar, and milk is added to the can—the cup top is jammed into place—and then the can is swung around and around the workman's head until he figures it's mixed enough. This done, the cup top is removed, filled with tea, and supped like ambrosia. What about the tea leaves?

What tea leaves? The contents are consumed with pleasure and contentment uncompared to anything in the world—and then back to work.

At night, a night watchman would keep the work area safe. He was normally a retired senior who didn't mind doing the boring, often cold job, of watching the work area for pilferers and vandals. He would sit in his hut, a small, portable hut just big enough to shelter him from the elements, and usually stare at the bright coke brazier while he drank his tea, ate his sandwiches and read yesterday's newspaper.

It was a lonely job, no one would ever speak to him, and of course his job meant he was working from 7 pm to 7 am. Occasionally if the work area was more than he could see from his chair or stool, he would get up and walk around to check things, often out of boredom and for something to do. Tar pots that flamed this way and that into the dark reaches of the night usually lit up the work area. If one of the tar pots ran out of tar, or the wind blew it out, the watchman would relight it—often the most exciting thing of his night. If anyone came near, he was usually sent on his way with a gruff rebuttal and a gesture—it was no place for a social interaction that was for sure.

When morning came, the night watchman would dissolve from view to wherever watchmen go in the daytime (probably underground) and reappear like magic the next night. I often wondered where the city found these thespians of the night. Was there a Nightwatchman's Union, or maybe a brotherhood of Night Purveyors?

Wherever they came from they were usually older, usually portly gentlemen, unshaven, poorly but warmly dressed, and scared little boys to death!

# 16. The Bus on the Sidewalk

Just for something to do differently, I decided to sit on the front step of our house in Cattell Road, Small Heath, Birmingham, and just watch the people going by to see what people do when they don't know you're watching them.

The number 54 bus ran down Cattell Road. Its route was from Stechford to Carrs Lane in the City Centre where I caught the bus to go home. The buses were cream and dark blue, the colours of the Birmingham City Motor Corporation.

The earlier ones were real boneshakers and the ride from town was anything but smooth. However, when the corporation brought out the new Daimler buses—well that was a cool ride. The best ride was upstairs, sitting over the top of the driver. Also you had a good view of everything. The worst was at the back on the three-seater in front of the emergency exit window at the back of the upstairs deck.

My friend showed me one day just how easily the window opened, and I often wondered if you would get trampled in the crush if it was ever needed to be used in an emergency.

At one time, my mother worked at the Coventry Road bus depot cleaning the buses. The cleaners stood on scaffold that ran alongside the buses and cleaned them by hand. My mother didn't like climbing the scaffold, and rather than climb down and then back up, she preferred to climb on to the top of the bus while the other workers moved the scaffold around the bus to the other side and then climb back on to the scaffold. The foreman thought she was crazy!

The bus drivers drove their buses like one of the four men of the Apocalypse—crazy, but accurate. How they manipulated those big buses around the small, tight corners I will never know.

One day, though, when the council workmen were tearing up the tramlines in the middle of Cattell Road, one bus driver tried to cut it a little too fine in his judgement of the distance of the roadwork to the curb.

I was sitting on the step watching the workmen, always a good pastime for kids, when the bus's front kerbside wheel mounted the sidewalk and the side of the bus hit the cast-iron light pole standard that was just to the side of our front door.

There was a tremendous bang as the bus caught the pole and the glass in the window next to the pole shattered and a huge piece of it fell in to the bus. Unfortunately, a woman had been sitting there and caught the full weight and force of the broken pane.

Safety glass is designed to shatter into small pieces, so after the initial wallop onto the top of her head, she was then showered with hundreds of shards of broken window.

The bus came to an immediate stop, still up the kerb, and the bus driver jumped out of his cab and ran around to see what had happened. Well, there was chaos, screaming, crying, and oh, lots of blood—lots and lots of blood! The bus conductor took charge and broke out the first aid kit and tried to assist the shocked lady who minutes before had been quietly reading her book. The ambulance was quickly there and the lady taken away to the hospital. The bus could not be moved until the police arrived and investigated so now besides the roadwork causing congestion, the bus had plugged up the one side of the road completely.

Goodness knows what the driver had to explain, I felt kind of sorry for him. The other passengers were moved to a replacement bus and the damaged one was eventually taken away to the garage.

# 17. Little Shop

I felt very proud of myself as I ran down the St. Benedict's School hill homewards.

Today, my Auntie Irene wasn't able to meet me to see me safely home, so as a 'big boy' I had been allowed to run home by myself just this one time—no talking to anyone.

I ran as fast as my little legs would let me, for today I had a special prize under my arm.

During class time at school, the young six year olds always had a plasticine time—a time when they rolled their lumps of plasticine into wonderful shapes, animals and monsters. The only problem with this was that the boards would get very dirty and sticky. Occasionally, when they were really dirty, the teacher would send each pupil home with their plasticine board for the mother of the house to wash it.

This was one of those days, except I had TWO boards. My special friend, Sheila Lowrey, was sick from school, so I had asked if I could take hers home too; I was sure my mother wouldn't mind washing two. The teacher had thought about it and decided it was all right to do this, so down the hill I ran, eager to show my special prize at home—two boards, what an honour!

When I reached the main road at the bottom of the hill, I had to turn sharp right and my house was the fifth on the right.

The house my parents rented was actually the top half of a beautiful Victorian villa home, very splendid in its time, now owned by the local council and rented to workers who needed subsidised rental homes as they couldn't afford the rents demanded by owners of private homes.

The house consisted of three stories, my parents rented the top two—well it wasn't really two, it was the second floor plus the attic on top where my brother and I slept. It was a typical attic; the beams of the gables showing in the room with a little triangular window covered in net curtain for privacy, with a bulb hanging from the beams on a long twisted wire. My mother was very frugal, so the bulb was only a few watts; just enough to see your way around.

The front of the house was very magnificent, with gorgeous stone steps leading up to a heavy panelled solid front door with a huge round cast-iron knob at its centre. The door would open like the gate of a fortress and close with a dull heavy thud.

Because it was so heavy, it was usually left open, pinned back by a piece of masonry.

Behind the doorway, was the large hallway, always present in Victorian homes. When the house was a single family home, the hallway lead to a stairway immediately opposite the main door that lead to the upper bedrooms and bathroom, while to the right of the hall was the main 'drawing room' with its splendid fireplace and huge floor to ceiling windows. Passing the drawing room, a passage led to the main dining room on the right, then the kitchen and then the scullery. Victorian homes always made full and good use or their hallways and passageways.

In modern times, a doorway had been put at the bottom of the stairs to partition off the upstairs living, with a similar door to the right to privatise the lower rooms for the tenants there.

I reached the steps at the front of the house with great enthusiasm and excitement. As I climbed the steps I suddenly realised, if Mom is at work, Auntie Irene (who rented the front two rooms of our flat) wasn't home, how would I get in? I knew that dad, a night-shift worker, would have gone to bed about seven or eight o'clock that morning, would be up by now, after all it was four thirty in the afternoon Well, the obvious thing was to ring the bell—so I did. No answer, so I rang again and again and again.

No reply whatsoever. Maybe the bell wasn't working today, sometimes it didn't. What should I do? I quickly came up with a solution. I banged on the door with relish and enthusiasm born of a little guy who has two plasticine boards to be washed.

No answer.

Well, nothing for it—I kicked the door until the sound echoed up the stairs for all to hear.

No answer.

What now? I espied the piece of masonry holding the front door open. That would do nicely.

I struggled with the large lump of rock and wrestled it over to the door at the bottom of the stairs. I lifted it as high as I could and threw it against the door.

BOOM! It hit the door with an unbelievably loud bang.

That done, I hauled it back to its usual place.

I had just done that when the door opened.

*Ah, finally,* I thought.

Standing at the open door with a face like thunder was my father looking like devil himself.

"What do you think you're doing?" he thundered in a loud stentorian voice, "Get in, and get upstairs, NOW!"

Taken a back at my father's angry voice, I suddenly realised my father must have still been in bed (at 4:30 in the afternoon?) and my rock had woken him up.

I needed no second bidding. I had heard my father sound like this before and it meant no good to anyone.

I ran to the stairs and up the wooden staircase as quickly as my little legs would carry me. I climbed with wings on my feet, clutching my precious plasticine boards under my arm. However, no matter how quickly I tried to scale the stairs, I was no match in strides to my father who was behind me in a flash, smacking me hard and furiously across the back of my thighs and bottom with the back of his large, powerful hand—literally driving me up the stairs with smacking power. No matter how I tried, I could not get far enough ahead to avoid the bad-tempered viciousness of my father awakened from his late sleep.

By the time I reached the top of the flight of stairs, I was hurting and bruised and stinging from my bottom down to my knees, and no matter how I cried, sobbed and pleaded, my father's onslaught followed me to the last step.

At this point, I was sobbing, shaking and tears ran down my face, flooding out beneath my round National Health spectacles and down my face.

I just wanted to get away from this inhuman onslaught from a person who supposedly was my father, someone who was supposed to love and protect me.

At the top of the stairs, my father thundered at me to get up to my room and stay there. I was only too pleased to oblige. I ran as fast as my battered little legs would carry me, up the curved staircase to the attic where I happily closed the door and sat on the edge of my iron bed with the flock mattress sobbing and wondering why my father had acted this way to toward me. I cried so hard that the little green candles ran down my face onto my lip and fell off at my chin onto my short pants.

I sat there for what seemed hours, until I heard the door at the bottom of the staircase open and the laughter and giggles of my younger brother.

My mother was home, oh good! I heard my mother and brother climbing the stairs below, laughing and enjoying each other's responses. My mother had picked my younger brother up from day care where he'd been while she was at work

This was better, soon my mom would come up to the attic and tell me everything was alright. She would explain to my dad that I was only doing what I thought was right, and then I would go down for tea and everyone would be happy again.

I sat there and waited and waited and waited—but no mom came. I had heard my father's dull, low voice mumbling in the kitchen and figured he was telling her what had happened.

I sat there on my bed, quiet, still, and cold. The light from the little window with the net curtain was dimming, it was getting late.

I realised I was hungry, but didn't dare make any move from my bed.

After what seemed like an eternity, I recognised the sound of my mother's footsteps on the staircase leading to the attic. Finally! She had come to get me for teatime.

The door creaked open and in the dim light I saw my mother come in carrying a little tray.

Now, everything would be alright—but why the tray?

My mother pushed the tray toward me saying, "You'd better stay up here, your dad's not too happy with you."

No hug? No kiss? No telling me it was OK?

Instead, without any comment, or reassurance, my mother picked up the plasticine boards and headed for the door.

"I need to go to the toilet," I pleaded.

"When you've finished eating that, brush your teeth in the bathroom, go to the toilet and then you'd better get into bed."

I was mortified! That was it? Even my Mother was being unkind to me. I sat on the edge of my bed, trying to eat my tea but it was going down in lumps.

It was finally dark. I was lying in my bed, covered by the sheet and blanket, when the door opened and in came my mother carrying my brother. She carried him over to his bed, tucked him in, kissed him and wished him good night and then headed toward the door. I waited for my mother to come over to me, give a kiss and hug like she had my brother, but she went straight to the door, closed it behind her and put the lock on the door, just in case my brother tried to get out; he was too young for stairs, especially as steep as they were and would have fallen all the way to the main floor.

I heard her go down the stairs, turn and head for the kitchen. I had been beaten, ostracised and now completely ignored by my own mother because of what my father had obviously said about me and what should be done about it.

If this was the way a mother and a father treated their first-born, what would tomorrow bring?

# 18. Frogspawn

Not far from where we lived at the Maypole, was a little brook that ran beside the school. It gurgled its way across the meadows and onto the farmland of Eileen Core's father. As Eileen and I were good friends, she would show me how the brook ran under the wire fence to keep the school kids out and onto the pond where all the frogspawn was.

Eileen was a freckle-faced girl with bunched red ringlets tied at the side of her head, and big teeth and always a grin.

Before we went to get the frogspawn, we would always spend time catching the little red-breasted fish in the brook. We never took anything to put them in so would satisfy our catching them and then letting them go.

It was Friday after school, and I had brought a jar with me this time. No ordinary jar, but a jar with a rim, around which I had tied some string to carry the jar by when I had it full of frogspawn.

We worked our way down the brook, under the wire and on to the mother load of frogspawn. So much! The frogs certainly liked this spot—it was everywhere and lots of it!

I stooped down and quickly filled my jar with the wonderful stuff—*lots of tadpoles here,* I thought.

I had to be off home before my mother realised I hadn't arrived home at the same time as the boy who lived next door to us.

As a proud hunter, with my trophy bubbling and slopping in my jar, I hurried up the road as quickly as I could—such a prize.

Now up the short gully way, past the Daley's house, onto the housing estate—soon be home.

As I walked up the last few yards to my house, I suddenly had a thought. My jar, with the looping string handle, reminded me of the tea cans I had seen the road workers holding when they had their tea. To make their tea, they would put the sugar, tea and milk into the can first, then add the water and to mix it all up; would take hold of the loop handle and whirl it around and around by the handle by the side of their bodies to make a nice cup of tea.

I had often seen this and wondered what it would be like to do this as the tea always tasted so good.

Well, hey, I had a jar, looked just like a tea can; it had a loop handle, so what was I waiting for? Go ahead and try it.

Seized by the moment, I grasped the handle and like the workmen I had seen, whirled it around the side of my body. The centrifugal force that held the workman's tea in the can held my frogspawn totally in place too. Well done. Hmmm, I only did it once though. The workmen do it a few times.

So here it goes for a second try, this time I'll try a few whirls—once, twice, thrice and...oops! All of a sudden, the weight of my jar on the string disappeared—at the same time I saw my precious jar of frogspawn arcing up, up, up into the air on a steep trajectory...and BOOM! It hit the road with an enormous explosive sound.

There, all over the road, running down the gutter was my precious load of frogspawn, dribbling to nothing on the hard, hot concrete.

The noise had been so loud, my mother came out to see what all the noise was about—horrified to see so much broken glass everywhere—never seeing my lost load of unborn frogs.

She quickly hurried me inside, asking what I was doing with the string I had in my hand.

"Oh…nothing."

Which is exactly what I had left after all my trouble and stupidity, guess I'll never make a workman.

# 19. The Boiled Ham Shop

In early times, councils hadn't yet realised the cash cow of little huxter store licences. The level of bureaucracy was such that anyone in Small Heath, in Birmingham could just up and open a store in the front room of their rented council house.

These houses opened right on to the sidewalk, no garden or grassed area; just open the front door and step onto the sidewalk. Although, residentially this did not make the front of the house very appealing, it was ideal if you had a business in the front room.

These little front room businesses ranged from china shops, grocery shops, mechanical spare parts, all the way to a bookie shop. Although the latter was illegal, everyone in the neighbourhood benefited from an occasional 'flutter' and so kept Mum about its presence, even to warning the operator if the police were around—more like a mutual benefit society.

One such shop was a little grocer's run by a lady called 'Rose.' She was a plump, dark haired lady with her trademark floral pinafore and always a big smile to greet you.

She ran the little 'uxter shop not far from where we lived, in fact just a few doors up from us. Our house front was up off the sidewalk by a few steps, but hers was at street level which made it more easily accessible for the public.

A different builder had obviously built her house at a different time to ours.

Instead of one large window, the front of her main window was made up of little panes of glass within wooden frames. This made her store look like one of David Copperfield's storefront. To enhance this, Rose had even put an occasional bottle bottom pane in it with its characteristic swirl.

Very eye-catching to see, but impossible to look through. The frames around these little panes had been painted white; contrary to the Victorian builder's 'drab brown,' as was the custom in Victorian times.

On the way to school, I would often see Rose standing at her counter talking to a customer, but she was never too busy to wave to me with a big smile as I passed. Rose was always happy; her jovial personality quite infectious, guaranteed to start your day off on a positive note.

One of the things that Rose sold was boiled ham, locally considered a luxury and a delicacy in the area at the time.

As such a delicacy was considered an excessive luxury, Rose had to make it appealing by presenting it in such a way as to allow the locals to 'justify' their spending their hard-earned money.

How did she do this? She shaved it so thinly; you could have spit through it. The ultra-thin slices of boiled ham were so thin as to be unrecognizable as boiled ham, you just knew it was boiled ham because the sign said so—more like pieces of saran wrap.

Her marketing technique was to write the 'special' price using a thick mixture of whitewash and a little paintbrush on one of her windowpanes in large letters with an exclamation mark after the price.

One of the things that Rose couldn't understand, no matter how many times people tried to explain to her, was that if she wrote the sign on the windowpane from inside her shop behind her counter, it was back to front from the road!

Many times we called her into the street to show her the reversal. She was always amazed and surprised to see it back to front.

She would always look a little puzzled and exclaimed, "But it's the right way round from inside the store, why is it back to front from the street?"

She just couldn't grasp the principal.

So, to keep Rose from fretting, someone would write the sign for her 'from the street side' and put a piece of card covering the pane from the inside. This stopped Rose worrying why her sign was back to front from inside the store, but more importantly, the sign was the right side round for the customers in the street.

This helped everyone in the area, especially Rose, who sold lots of boiled ham.

# 20. Dolly's Pram

The place was Birmingham, England, the year 1950. I was a little boy of 6, following along behind my mom on the way to the stores.

The war had been over for five years now, but everywhere you looked there were piles of rubble and bombed buildings; a true witness to the carnage and destruction that the Luftwaffe had wrought on the people of Birmingham in their desperate search for munition factories and fabrication factories which had worked 24/7 to resupply the men fighting at the front with new war material as the battles took their toll.

Birmingham, with its reputation of a city of a thousand trades, had been hit hard as the German echelon knew that the town had many factories that would help their cause if they could be destroyed.

What the German bomber command never realised, is that Birmingham, as an industrial city had not evolved like other cities such as Manchester or London, where the industrial areas are all together; in Birmingham, they were all around the outskirts of the city.

As such, they were all over the place and a real pain to the bombers trying to find the 'mother load' of factories.

The German bombers were successful on some nights, but in many cases, it was more by luck than judgement— the bombers just dumping their bombs to get rid of them as the fuel ran low and heading home for the safety of the European mainland.

This meant that many of these bomb loads, dropped in fear or panic, fell not on an industrial area but in many cases civilian residential areas, like the area where my house was.

As a matter of fact, a load of bombs fell on the maternity home where I was born when I was three days old.

This meant that even five years after the war, there were bombed sites everywhere. It was common to see a huge space in a row of houses, with the walls at the second and third story hanging out into space, showing the burned wallpaper of what had been someone's pride and joy living room, now a charred hulk of yesterday.

These sites were still open, not fenced or closed off to stop kids going in there. It was an austere time in Britain, and there were no eggs, sugar, chocolate and certainly no money for fences.

The sites were always covered in the flower called Morning Glory. It seemed the alkaline soil resulting from the bomb explosion was ideal for their growing. So, everywhere you looked, were white flowers blooming in abundance. The sites were our playgrounds, no fears of the site and its potential hazard of exposed wires from the mains.

No one had cleared these sites or inspected them; they were still the same as when the bomber had left. In many cases, long wooded props were holding up bulging walls that had lost their support from the house next door.

Such was the environs, as I tripped along behind my mother as she threaded her way along the narrow streets of Victorian row houses, with their leached red brick walls and blue slate roofs.

The women we passed still wore headscarves all the time. Not because it was cold, but rather by a five-year habit, as they had always had to use the headscarf as a 'turban' when they worked in the munition factories to keep their long hair from getting caught in the machine they were working on.

We passed the 'baths' on the left with its roof still missing, covered by a big tarp. The 'baths' were actually the place where the workers came to take a bath on Friday night after the week's work to get themselves clean for the weekend.

The cost was one penny, two pennies if you wanted soap and a towel. Next door to these baths, they had renovated the area just prior to the war and made a swimming pool (the swimming baths).

The latter had received a direct hit, the bomb landing right in the middle of the pool. If I bent down and squinted through the keyhole, I could still see the debris in the bottom of the pool.

Next to the baths was the local library, still intact in all its Victorian splendour with a high tower at the end (this is now the local Mosque).

The road we were on joined the main road at about a forty-five-degree angle. This meant that where it joined the main road, it formed a triangular piece of ground at the juncture of the two roads.

At this juncture, there had been a store that sold shoes. It, too, was now a bombsite, and being triangular was a bit awkward to negotiate to get around to the other side. To keep the public out and to make it safe, someone had erected a high fence of wooden pickets with wire strung between the pickets.

Everywhere you looked on the site was the remains of the store's interior, burned and blackened with charred wood showing at the openings that now remained. Add to this the presence of large piles of grey ash, and the whole ambience of the site was very sorrowful.

The building had been two-story, so the upstairs floors hung down into the lower floor like bones of a dinosaur, just waiting to fall down.

As my mother and I navigated this 'heritage' site to get onto the main road, I noticed behind the fence, among the rubble that had been pushed back against the walls for safety, a little girl's doll's pram.

It had been a maroon colour, but now covered in ash and dust and burned on the one corner, it sat sadly in its place, twisted and abandoned.

Immediately, my heart leapt into my chest. If the doll's pram was there, where was the little girl who had owned this treasure?

Had she been at home in the air raid shelter when the bomb dropped?

Had someone just found the pram after a raid and thrown it over the fence to get it out of the way?

Had the little girl been pushing her dolly in it when the bomb dropped and she....

This was too hard and sad to think about. I asked my mother what had happened to her.

She just looked at me and said, "Her mommy would have taken care of her."

But what did that really mean?

The bombsite, the fence and the burned dolly's pram stayed there for years.

Every time I went by, I asked myself the same question over and over, but could never come up with an answer.

Then one day when I went past, the remains of the bombed building were gone—gone forever. The workmen had come, taken down the fence, removed the debris, dolly's pram and all, pulled down the building and on the triangular site there was just blacktop.

The flat, black triangular mark, joining the two sidewalks of the streets was all that remained of the history of the building.

The eyesore was gone, but so was dolly's pram and my long-awaited question—what happened to the little girl.

I have since talked to people who lived in the area. Not only can they not remember a dolly's pram being there, they don't remember the burned building with the fence around.

So, if you talk to a woman someday, who sadly remembers losing her dolly in an air raid in Small Heath, Birmingham, at the junction of Green Lane and Coventry Road, maybe you could let me know.

Otherwise, I'll always wonder....

# 21. The Toilet Cistern

The house we lived in in Birmingham, England had been built in 1875. As it was now 1954, that made the house about 79 years old. Most things of 79 years old are ready to quit. Oh no, the Birmingham Council reckoned for at least another 25 years.

This meant that we were living in a house with early Victorian technology, or NOT; there was no technology. As a heart of the industrial revolution, Birmingham had been developed on a make-do-and-mend-for-today attitude to get houses up for the workers coming in from the country.

The attitude of the councils exemplified the attitude that whatever the 'peasant' were given, it was far better than they had been used to.

The problem was, 79 years later, the tenants of the houses were still expected to cope with out-of-date ideas that didn't work in 1875, and certainly didn't work now.

Take for example, the flush toilet. This had been a big step forward from the bucket latrine form at the turn of the century. Not a nice subject you say. OK, but it is a fact of life. Flushing into the main sewer, was considered just as much a technological leap as the iPod from a gramophone.

However, in 1954, the same principle was used as in 1875. To wit: a toilet sat on the blue brick floor in the toilet, outside in the yard, with a door covering the opening with a wide ventilation space above and below the door. This was enough to give adequate privacy.

Arising from the back of the toilet, was a large bore pipe down which the water would pour and flush the toilet contents into the sewer.

But, how did the water get into the pipe?

About six feet off the floor was the cistern. A cast-iron container holding about ten gallons of water connected to this down pipe.

Now, getting the water down the pipe was the trick of the early Victorian technology.

The down pipe protruded up into the cistern until it was nearly level with the top (are you understanding this word picture?). Sitting over this, was a bell-shaped housing, which just sat there resting on the bottom of the cistern. Next to the housing sat a ball cock, a device that rose when the water came into the cistern and closed the water valve when the ball cock was level with the top of the cistern.

To flush the toilet, you pulled on a chain which caused the bell housing to lift up, pulling the water upwards from the vacuum formed and dumped the water down the pipe flushing the toilet.

How simple you say. Yes, but if the ballcock arm was not properly aligned, it meant that the water would not completely turn off. This made an annoying seep of water all the time, which was very distracting to the participant.

Now you know how it works, here's my story.

One Saturday night, my parents had gone out so we were all by ourselves. No TV, no radio and I'd read all the comics. What was a ten-year-old to do?

*I know,* I thought, *I'll fix that drippy toilet. All I have to do is bend the arm and the ballcock will be higher and stop that seepage and annoying sound.*

So, into the toilet I go. Jump up on the wooden seat, lift the cover up—oh, such a simple job!

I reached into the murky tank, full of rusty water and chunks of rust and grabbed the ball cock arm. Here goes! I twisted the copper arm up and let it go to see the result of my work. Oh darn! Now the water was rushing in, I'd bent it the wrong way! Quickly, I grabbed it again and twisted it back the other way to compensate for my wrong twist the first time.

Do you know what happens when you bend a copper rod one way and then quickly the other way? Yes, it breaks!

Now there was no control at all by the ball cock, and the water came rushing into the cistern at mains pressure. In a flash, the cistern was full, very full, and the water was pouring over the edge of the cistern and onto the floor— across the floor and into the yard! There was water everywhere and it sounded like Niagara Falls! Panic!

I quickly tried to close the valve through which the water was coming, but when the copper rod broke it only left about an inch of rod left attached to the valve. No matter how I tried, I didn't have enough strength to close the valve.

By now, I had a tidal wave pouring into the yard. It was dark outside and I couldn't see just where the water was going. Was it going toward the drain, or the back door of the house? What was I going to do?

I thought frantically! No ball cock, no parent and no help—I really was up the creek without a paddle.

I suddenly remembered that once I had noticed a water shut-off by the front door in the sidewalk.

I ran like an idiot to the front side of the house and found the shut-off in the dark. The cover hadn't been opened for years, but desperation and fear took care of that. I plunged my hand into the cavity below the cover—a tap! I grabbed it and cranked it in the off direction. When I could crank no more, I stopped and listened. Niagara Falls seemed to have stopped.

I ran back to the toilet and sure enough all was quiet—for a brief minute.

"Who's turned the water off?" comes a booming voice from the back house at the bottom of our garden (at nine o'clock at night).

It was Mrs. Pickering.

"Who turned the water off?" the booming, stentorian voice came again. I was terrified!

"It's me, Mrs. Pickering," I lamented.

"You naughty boy, turn it back on!" she demanded.

"I can't," I appealed.

"I need to use the toilet, now turn it on! Just wait until I see your dad, he'll be really mad!"

Oh no, my dad, Mrs. Pickering and a broken ball cock arm, what could be worse—death?

I tried to tell her but she was adamant.

"If it's not on in five minutes, I'm coming round to turn it on myself," she threatened.

OK, so I've got five minutes, after which all life ends for me!

I tried to think of what I could do in five minutes to fix this mess.

A brilliant idea came to mind. I ran into the house and grabbed a roll of copper wire my dad had under the sink.

With this, I bound the remaining short end of the ball cock arm against the valve and hoped it was tight enough.

I then quickly ran down to the shut-off and gingerly turned it on. No sound of Niagara—yet.

I ran back to the toilet and behold, my engineering feat had worked, and it wasn't leaking. 'Phew,' no more Mrs. Pickering to deal with—but what about my dad?

The water-dripping problem was taken care of but that also meant you couldn't flush the toilet. Never mind, one thing at a time.

Just as I was congratulating myself, I heard the sound of my parents' footsteps.

Oh boy, no I'm in trouble.

My parents came through the back door and saw me standing in the yard, surrounded by water.

"What are you doing? You're all wet," my mother questioned.

What was I to say; this night couldn't get any worse.

"Er, I was using the toilet and the cistern broke, and I used some of Dad's wire to fix it," I offered.

"Oh, what a clever boy you are! Good job, you were here when it happened," my mother replied.

Well, I hadn't actually told a lie, and for once, my parents were looking at me proudly. Or was it just the Guinness they had enjoyed that evening.

Who cares? Saved my hide—and a go-round with Mrs. Pickering.

# 22. Little Edie

It was Friday morning in Jamaica Row, in Birmingham, market day with my Uncle Jack.

We were at the toast and jam and cup of tea stage, waiting for the porter to tell us everything was loaded in the van.

It was a bitterly cold morning, not quite winter, but cold enough. I was warming my hands on my mug in preparation to going outside to brave the elements to go back to the van.

The coffee shop was full as usual, everyone pushing and shoving to get to the counter to get his hot drink and toast. The sound in there was a busy, jovial kind of sound; everyone bustling to get their business done and on their way once they'd had a cuppa.

I had eaten half of my toast and most of my tea when a frail, little old lady emerged through the doorway, looked to see if the owner had seen her and made her way quietly to the far corner where we sat by the heater.

She looked up and her faded grey eyes smiled a weak, faint greeting as the moved to sit on the seat behind me. From that position, the owner couldn't see her and she was in a nice snug place to keep warm.

"Hello," I said through a mouthful of toast and jam, "What's your name?"

"Edie," she replied, "Edie Smith."

"Mine's Bill," I replied, "You look cold."

I saw that she had a thin summer frock on that had seen much better days, covered by her Salvation Army coat, well-worn but still keeping her warm on this frosty morning. The coat itself would have been warm but she had no scarf to go with it, or mittens to keep her blue hands warm.

She sat quietly by the heater and kept fingering her lapel, which I noticed, had a burn or scorch mark on it. She was obviously very conscious of this burn mark and was trying to hide it, its presence showing her poverty.

When I looked down, I saw that she had no socks or stockings on; just bare feet, blue with cold, in old shoes whose high heels had been cut down to the sole to give her something to walk on.

This little old lady was a sorry sight to me, who sat there with a big doorstep of toast and a hot drink, and not the first one today.

I saw her look longingly at my toast and then look away politely. It occurred to me that she hadn't eaten for a while and was just skin and bones beneath that coat.

I looked at her carefully, and said, "Wow, I'm really full now! It seems a shame to waste this piece of toast with all that jam on it, would you like it?"

She looked longingly again at my plate, and then graciously looked away and said, "No thank you, I'm not really hungry."

She may have been poor, but she had lots of pride. Thoughts flashed before me as to how she must have looked as a pretty young teenager, a young woman and maybe someone's mum at one time.

"Well, I tell you what," I said, "I'll just leave it here in case you change your mind, I just don't want to waste such good food. This tea in my mug is much too much for me to drink, I'll leave that here too."

"Come on," my Uncle Jack had finished reading his paper and stood up to go, not aware of little Edie sitting between me and the heater.

"Are you bringing that toast? You can eat it on the way?" Uncle Jack queried.

"No, I've had enough, and I think Edie might like it," I responded.

"Who? Oh, come on," and away Uncle Jack strode.

Now that we were moving away from the table the owner would be soon coming to clean the tabletop in readiness for the next customer to sit there.

I saw Edie's hand reach out and gladly seize the toast and munch right into it; a look of luxury and ecstasy showing in those faded eyes. She probably hadn't had such a feed in a long time. She glugged the remains of the tea, and suddenly her dark, sombre little world looked better for the next while.

She stood up, now smiling, made her way to the door and disappeared into the black murk of the morning armed with resilience and fortitude to face another day.

We went to the coffee shop many times after that but never saw Edie again.

I always wondered, did she find her toast and tea somewhere else, or did her frailty finally overcome her fight for life, and she surrendered to the escape of this world one cold, dark night as she lay dreaming of toast and tea on her bed of newspapers and old clothes?

I asked around the coffee shops over time, but no one else remembered seeing Edie.

I just figure she was a special angel who flitted through my life that day and left me a memory for all time.

# 23. The Outdoor at the Pub

Sometimes, when my Grandfather went for a drink down the hill to The Brookhill, he went by himself. It was just a short walk, all down-hill on the way but all uphill on the way home, full of beer and oysters from the little van that waited outside the pub.

"Are you coming, Honor?" my Grandfather asked impatiently as he tied his silk cutter around his neck—the height of fashion somewhere in his life, and he still enjoyed wearing it.

"No, not tonight," my Grandmother replied, "Maybe I'll come and get a jug of draught beer later, but not now."

My Grandfather rolled his eyes, he'd already waited a half hour and he'd miss the beginning of the dominoes tournament; he was a contender.

So, off he went with a spring in his step, already imagining the winnings in his pocket.

A couple of hours later, my Grandmother finally decided she was ready for a good drink of draught beer and took the stone flagon out of the pantry from off the concrete slab.

She strolled down the hill toward the Brookhill and headed for the door marked 'outdoor;' the only place in the pub where you could take beer out by buying it retail over the counter.

"Pint of bitter," she offered to the bar tender standing behind the little counter in the outdoor.

"OK, Honor," he replied, "Your old man's doing well tonight in the dominoes tournament, winning everything to this point."

"That should please him," she smiled, "He could do with the extra cash, the television licence is due."

"Actually," said the bar man, "it's just about over; they'll be leaving in a minute, maybe he'll carry your beer up the hill for you."

"No he won't, he's not getting his hands on my beer."

She paid for the beer, checking there was not too much froth on the beer and she hadn't been short served on her measure. With a satisfied look, she turned on her heel and out of the door she went.

Just as she was leaving, she noticed that Grandfather 'Tom' was leaving by the main doors, looking very happy with himself and jingling the money in his trouser pocket.

But, right behind him came three men, the names of which she didn't know—strangers in the area.

Grandmother noticed they were striding after him with intent on their faces. Before she could say anything, two of the men grabbed my Grandfather while the third drew back his fist to hit him.

"Not the father of my children, you don't," Grandmother cried and hit the would-be assailant fair and square on the side of the head with the full pitcher of beer.

Down he went like a log! Grandmother swung around with the broken pitcher handle in her hand and took a second swing at one of the other men holding my Grandfather.

He had seen what happened to the first man and let go of my Grandfather and ran for his life.

Grandfather took care of the other man with his free fist.

They both stood there surveying the battleground, the first man still out like a light, covered in beer, the second groaning on the ground holding his jaw.

"Now look what you've made me do with my beer!" My Grandmother countered, "And it cost me sixpence!"

"Here, Honor," my Grandfather replied, plunging his hand into his full pocket of winnings, "buy yourself a couple of bottles."

So, up the hill they went, my Grandfather jingling his money, my Grandmother clutching her valuable two bottles of Guinness—what a night!

# 24. The Two Shillings Piece

It was Saturday morning, and very early at that—not even light yet. My uncle was putting a thermos of hot tea in his fishing creel and then we were off down the road to catch the bus to Stratford on Avon.

It was fishing day! I guess William Shakespeare was so busy being a verger and chasing Ann Hathaway, he never knew what he was missing right at his door. His father lived just across the way from the church that took up most of his time (until he met Ann) and the best coarse fishing in the county was right in front of his church.

We had to hurry down the hill to the bus stop so as not to miss the next bus. It was quite a walk across the town of Birmingham to get to the train station at Snow Hill, so we needed to have time on our side when we did.

We reached the bottom of the hill just as the bus came around the bend at the top of Alum Rock Road.

"On you go!" My uncle nodded, and then he swung on behind me. The conductor gave him a two-penny ticket and we were off to the town.

The daylight was just peeping through when we arrived at the city centre, and off we went to Snow Hill. Uncle Bert had his creel on a strap that he hung across his shoulder, the other hand held the long, narrow bag that protected his fishing rods—very personal piece of equipment.

He strode away, and I had a time keeping up with him. It was obvious that Uncle Bert could imagine already the fish on his line, "Come on Bill, we need to get there quickly."

Eventually, we reached Colmore Row and the steep steps that led down to the tracks of Snow Hill station.

Uncle Bert paid for his train ticket. The guard punched a hole in it with his special pliers and we were on to the station platform. I didn't need a ticket as I was too young.

The big, thick doors of the train hung open for us to choose our carriage and compartment. No sooner had we found a seat that the 'crunch' of the big doors closing on the carriage signalled we were about to take off.

The guard appeared from the guard's van at the back of the train, waved his green flag at the driver, blew his whistle and away we went.

Slowly at first, as the train driver let the steam valve open to get the huge engine moving, but then little by little we were gathering speed and leaving the station. A huge blast of the train whistle signalled we were off, and Stratford here we come.

As the train left the station, the first thing it did was go into a long underground tunnel. As it did so, the lights in the carriage came on so we could see what was going on.

"Close the window while we're in the tunnel," my Uncle offered. I had been standing on the seat looking out of the window.

The reason was soon obvious. I was a little slow getting the window closed and into the carriage came huge smut from the engine, like a big silent shadow.

My Uncle batted it away, and we waited while the train went through the tunnel. I thought the smell of the engine, a mixture of smoke and steam, smelled kind of nice but everyone else pulled a face.

We burst out of the tunnel into the Warwickshire countryside, and we were now well on our way. I liked the sound the train made when the bogies of the carriage went over the rail joins, 'bedump, bedump! bedump, bedump!', I still think of it today. It makes that characteristic noise when the wheels go over the join in the tracks because the joins are level. In North America, the joins are staggered.

In a short time, we reached Stratford. We were off that train like a whippet. My uncle told me we had to get to our fishing spot early, before someone else go there before us. After all, it was the best spot in Stratford!

On the way to the river, we had to detour to the fishing shop to get our maggots for bait.

My uncle had a round shallow tin with holes in the lid. He bought a pint of maggots that were quickly put in the tin and we were away.

We took the short cut down the church side of the river. I couldn't see how we were going to get across the river to our spot, when Uncle Bert stepped off the road and headed down the bank. I followed wondering where he was going.

In the early morning gloom, I had not seen the little, flat-bottomed boat waiting by the bank of the river. It was like a big punt, attached to a chain that went from the bank on this side of the river to the other side.

My uncle gave the man a penny and we both jumped on to the boat and sat on the raised edge. The man started to turn a big iron handle that somehow rolled the chain through a sprocket and he literally 'wound' the boat across the river.

Once on the other side, I jumped onto the bank, my uncle catching up behind. From here, it was not far at all to our spot.

'Our spot,' was special as it was next to the big weeping willow by the lock opposite the church. This weeping willow was a lifesaver when it started raining (which it did often). We would set the rods on the rod rests at the edge of the river and retreat under the willow where we could still see the float bob if a fish took the bait

The lock hadn't been used for years. It was green and slimy and all gunked up with river garbage so there was no fear of river traffic interfering with our fishing. We could sit there in peace and enjoy the day. My uncle kept his maggots active to attract the fish by holding them under his top lip against his teeth (really!)—made them wriggle more!

Today was not a premium day. Few bites and lots of rain. I was getting bored and tired. After all, I was only five.

I sat on Uncle's creel under the tree with a blanket around me.

Leaning against the tree, I soon fell asleep and when I did stir, Uncle Bert said, "How about if you go to the lady in the hut and get us a flask of tea?"

Sounded good to me! Uncle Bert pointed to a small cabin/hut just a little way away across the green field and gave me a two-shilling piece.

"Now then," he said, "Go to the window, knock on it and when the lady comes, give her the thermos flask and tell her you want tea with milk in it."

I grasped the two-shilling piece in my little hand. "Now, hold on tightly to that money, it's my last two shillings," he said as I set off—money in one hand, flask in the other.

I arrived at the window of the tea hut but it was closed. I banged on the window with my money hand to attract someone's attention.

The tea lady came to the window.

"Tea with milk in it, please," I said.

"O.K., O.K.," said the lady a little testy.

She held her hand out for the money. As I reached up to give it to her, the most terrible thing in the world happened.

As I reached up, my hand banged against her hand, and I dropped the two shillings.

The coin dropped down, down, down onto the deck in front of the window. But this was no ordinary deck.

The deck had slatted planks on it, and as I watched, my uncle's precious two shillings rolled across a board and fell into the space between the slats! I grabbed frantically but the evasive money fell through the decking onto the ground below—lost forever as there was no way to get under the deck, it was too close to the ground!

"Sorry, can't give you any tea without the money," the lady said and closed the window, leaving me standing on the deck, empty flask in one hand and no money, no change, in the other.

What was I going to tell Uncle Bert?

I walked back to the river and the willow very, very slowly.

When I arrived, you could see the anticipation in Uncle Bert's face as he imagined the taste of his tea.

I falteringly told him what had happened.

"What!" he cried, "So, now I have neither tea nor money, and I certainly don't have any more I can spare for tea. Oh, dear, what shall we do?"

I felt awful about the whole thing. Uncle Bert had trusted me, and I had let him down.

He walked back with me to the tea place to see if he could recover his money but soon realised it was a hopeless case. The slat spaces were too thin to 'angle' for the money, and the deck was only about a foot off the ground, so without ripping up a plank of the deck there was no way to recover the tea money.

The lady came to the window and seemed to think the whole thing quite funny. I didn't, and my uncle soon made it obvious he didn't either.

"There must be a fortune under that deck," she said, "You'd be surprised how many people lose their money that way."

My thought was, if that was the case, why hadn't she put a solid top on the deck to prevent that?

She told us that the building was leased, so not her business.

So, we didn't catch any fish, we didn't have any tea and went home 'water whacked' as the term is.

Many years later, when I was grown, I went to see if I could still yet recover the lost two shillings from under the deck and give it back, finally, to Uncle Bert.

Alack, Alas, when I arrived there, after taking the little wooden boat (that was now a new, little wooden boat) I found that the parks committee in their wisdom had redesigned the area and yes, you guessed it, had removed the building altogether—the building, the deck and worst of all, my uncle's two shillings!

Someone must have made a fortune!

# 25. Sweaty Feet

My father did a lot of labouring work in his life. This meant he was on his feet a lot. The result of this was—yes—lots of sweaty feet. But not just ordinary sweaty feet, these were mega, mega sweaty feet.

His feet perspired so much, he could only wear shoes made of leather to let his feet breathe—or so he told us.

He told me this had started when he was in France in the war. Now, I think you can blame the French for Marie Antoinette, good wine and some good cheese—ah, cheese, that's it!

His feet used to smell like really, really old cheese that had been in the dungeon for centuries.

It was so bad, that wherever he left his socks when he took them off, in a short while, the socks would be stiff and erect—gross!

This was no ordinary sweat, this was grade A, rot your socks sweat—literally.

If he didn't wash them right away, they would rot away and go into holes in a day or so.

Now, can you imagine what it must have been like at my Grandmother's? Four sons, all with potentially lethal sweaty feet—let me out of there!

My father used to wash his feet in permanganate of potash—guaranteed to cure—but not my father. All he ended up with was yellow feet.

We found out that the sweat of my father's feet neutralised the tannin in the leather and was the cause of the intense smell. The neutralised tannin would seep through the shoes and leave stains on the outside of the shoe.

So, although he needed leather to let his feet breathe, the very leather shoes were the cause of his problem.

Then came the day—gore-tex—finally a material that could breathe, but no tannin to be seen.

What a saving grace! At last, we could breathe normally! No stiff socks, no smell and no yellow feet. Isn't science wonderful?

# 26. The Gang

I was just nine years old when I moved to Cattell Road in Small Heath, Birmingham. Before this, we had lived in the country in a post war prefab with a beautiful rural ambience of green fields, hedgerows, lots of songbirds and bubbling brooks.

Now, Small Heath was quite different to this. The rural ambience was replaced by rows of joined villa houses of brick, built in 1875, now pock marked from years of pollution, smoke, dirt and general disrepair. The hedgerows were now the block long sidewalks of cracked paving stones, culminating in the gutter full of debris from the countless trucks and buses, plus whatever else had been thrown there.

Now the songbirds took the shapes of what seemed like millions of pigeons, along with the Starlings that came in huge flocks that blocked out the sun as the sun set. The noise of these Starlings in the night kept a lot of people awake—the pigeons fouling everything with guano.

Bubbling brooks? Well, that would be the torrents of water rushing down the gutter after a rainstorm; the swirling, muddy eddies blocking the drains and creating huge flood pools for the buses to swish through and soak anyone within ten feet! The trees were replaced by power poles that still held the overhead wires that powered the now obsolete trams—the dinosaur rails still embedded in the road.

To the 'natives' of Small Heath, this was 'normal.' To me, it was awful; having enjoyed the country and finding frogspawn, nests and baby Cuckoos. We did have a few crows but their 'song' was hardly melodious, rather coarse and raucous.

This was the time of crew cuts, drainpipe trousers and long suede coats—the teddy boy era.

My mother warned me, that the boys dressed like this were not nice, aggressive and potentially dangerous. After all, they carried knives, knuckle-dusters and chains!

This was so different to my previous lifestyle, that I was intrigued by the differences and curious at the total lifestyle now living around me.

I had noticed a family across the road from us. There were two boys and one girl. The older boy, about fourteen, was dressed in the 'teddy boy' clothes, and despite what my mother had said, I thought he looked very smart—as obviously did the girls hanging around him. His younger brother, whose name I found out was Lance, was about my age. His sister ran away when she saw me watching.

I had been idly looking across at them, not trying to be obvious about it when a bus passed in front of me, blocking them from my view.

As the bus passed, there the two brothers were—standing right in front of me.

"Hello!" said the older brother, "What's your name?"

They took me completely by surprise.

Not knowing what to say I just opened my mouth and a weak 'Bill' came out.

"We noticed you moved here just, and we were wondering if you'd like to join our gang."

Gang! Oh no! The mental pictures of knives, chains and knuckle-dusters came to mind.

Gang! What would my mother say?

"I don't know," I stammered, "I've never been in a gang before."

"Nothing to it," Lance offered, "just say yes, and we'll get you voted in."

"Voted in what?" I asked.

"The gang of course," Lance replied, "we have to make sure the rest of the gang agree, we can't just have anyone in our gang. Our territory goes from the end of the road by the Atlas Pub, down to the football grounds."

As soon as I heard the word 'territory' my mind filled with what I had heard from the movies about Al Capone and the mafia.

Oh, no. What would my mother say?

"I'll have to ask my mom," I spluttered.

"If you do, she'll say no I can tell you now," Lance replied, "but suit yourself, we'll ask you again tomorrow. By the way, this is not a fighting gang; more like security. This is a rough neighbourhood, and you need friends like us to make sure you're safe when you go out, especially at night."

Ah, I thought, no machine guns and black cars—good. Security sounds much better than gang. At this point in my life, I had never been in a real fight and the thought of such a thing made me a little weak at the knees.

I decided to see for myself. So, when night came, I snuck down the entry and stood in the shadows of the entry and watched the road.

I now saw quite a few of the 'gang'—different ages from about twelve to about twenty. They stood together on the other side of the road just talking among themselves; not noisy or crass, just a bunch of teenagers enjoying the time together.

Suddenly, I saw a group of 'outsiders' coming down the road, dressed in dark clothes with the crepe-soled shoes of teddy boys.

When they saw the 'gang,' they quietly and inconspicuously put what they had in their hands in their pockets, crossed over to the other side of the road, looked straight ahead and floated past the entry where I was not making a sound.

The 'gang' just watched them silently and waited until the intruders were in the 'safe' zone out of their territory.

Police were far and few in this part of the city, and so seeing the safe situation they had caused make me feel good about living in this new house. At least now, I could go to the local store or newsagent and not be afraid of every dark doorway or missing light from the streetlights.

I decided in my youthful wisdom not to ask my mother. I would just tell her I had met some friends.

The next day, I told Lance and his brother I would join, but I had to be discreet as my Mother wouldn't agree. They told me that was fine.

I asked about the 'intruders' from last night.

"Oh yes, they're from the Bordesley Green area, had a bit of trouble with them but we sorted them out. They're allowed to pass through, but not stop," Lance offered.

"But you told me there was no fighting," I protested.

"Well...sometimes we have to, just to keep our demarcation lines clear," Lance explained.

*Oh, no* I thought, *now I've really gone and done it.*

Lance further explained, "It's like the Russians with their ultimate deterrent. We make them realise it could just be unhealthy if they mess with us. Oh, by the way, did we tell you about the training sessions?"

"Training what?" I queried, "Is this more fighting?"

"Oh no," Lance began, "it's just training in case we ever do need to fight the others. An older brother of one of the gangs was a Marine, and he's promised to show us a few things."

Now I knew I was in it up to my neck. I didn't have the courage to ask what a person had to do to leave the gang. Maybe if I had, they would have used me for practice.

So, as the weeks passed I spent a lot of time with my 'friends' and learned very quickly the finer points of street fighting. My mother was so pleased to see me mixing with the local kids. If only she'd known.

I seemed to have a hidden natural aggression, and quickly gained respect from some of the hardliners.

"I thought you said you never fought," one of the older members mentioned.

"I didn't," I answered truthfully.

"Well, in that case, you're a natural."

Besides learning the street hit and run methods, I also learned how to find my way through the maze of streets, back house yard entries and the most fantastic thing of all—how to vault over a six-foot wall when you're being chased—especially by the police.

These rival gangs around us had not missed 'manoeuvres' that we were taking part in. It seemed to them we must be preparing for 'war.'

To this extent, they kept well away from us and offered no trouble. Even went along streets that took them around us rather than passing through. The scenario kind of reminded me of the movie 'Tombstone' where the Earp brothers kept the town quiet and clean.

These new found 'skills' gave me a personal confidence I had never had before, and I would walk out at night and never worry.

When I was about eleven years old, I passed what was known as the Eleven Plus exam. This meant I would be going to a grammar school out of our district, while my peers would be staying in the local area to go to school.

I felt sorry that I would not see my friends at school, and by passing this exam, I had moved 'up in the world' into a higher class of learning. Along with this, went the promise of my leaving the working class, factory work and a smart uniform, shiny shoes and a leather satchel to carry my books—all foreign to my Small Heath friends. Instead of resenting me for this, the gang wished me well and offered me their best in escaping from the drudgery of the area that they and their parents were trapped in—had been for generations.

They told me I was still in the gang and not to forget it.

The months passed, and my homework and long journey to school kept me off the streets and seeing my gang friends. I would occasionally see one or two as I stepped down from the bus and always waved.

One night, I was late from school and it was dark by the time I arrived at my stop. Now, this stop was just over our gang's boundary and thus in another gang's area.

As I stepped off the bus, there was a whole bunch of this area's gang members hanging around the stop. They immediately recognised me and started to sneer and call names to me.

I was outnumbered something like fifteen to one, so I tried to ignore them and walk as quickly as I could, without showing panic, toward the boundary of their area and our gang's area.

I knew that once I crossed the magic line, they would leave me alone.

However, they knew this and before I reached the magic boundary, some of them intentionally stood in front of me to block my passage.

Their taunts grew louder, trying to get me to react and then they would have been on me like a pack of wolves.

I was just about to abandon ship and make a whirling dervish suicide attempt at the closest ones—take a few with me before they got me—when I heard what sounded like the chink of a chain.

The sound came from behind the gang members in front of me that were blocking my way.

The members turned to look behind them and gasped in fear.

There stood about twenty members of our gang, complete with chains, knuckle-dusters and open razors— the kind I had only seen pictures of until now.

151

"Problem?" the question coming from our supreme gang member, a big guy called Tommy Newey.

"Oh, no, no, not at all," said the individual in front of me, who had been mouthing off to me a few minutes before, quaking in his boots seeing our gang in full battle mode. "Just wanted to make sure he got home safely."

A big expletive beginning with 'F' exploded from Tommy's mouth and the gang took one step forward.

My hecklers from the other gang were gone in a flash like smoke in a chimney.

"Nice to see you again," I said, very thankful for their timely appearance, "Glad you were around. Thanks, I really appreciate what you did."

"Hey," said Tommy, "you're still one of us, and we take care of our own."

So the gang took me home to my door. It must have seemed a strange sight—me in my posh uniform and satchel being chaperoned by a gang of street fighters.

But hey, these are my friends.

# 27. Toilet Paper

Ultra-soft, pillow top, double absorbent—what does that bring to mind? Sheets? Beds? Bandages? How about toilet paper?

In today's society, these are the choices we have to make when shopping at our local supermarket—oh, the stress! So many toilet papers, and so little time before we have to get home and watch the news!

Wasn't always like this.

I think back to post war Britain and the shortages and sacrifices that were made that most modern people couldn't even bear to think about.

When it was time to go to the La Pom, it was sometimes out in the yard—a brick-built cubicle with a 'farm' gate as a door, spaces above and below the door, just a piece of wood protecting modesty and called a door.

Like all projects in life, it's not over until the paperwork is done!

This was not as easy as it may sound.

'Toilet paper' was the daily newspaper torn into squares, pushed onto a small 'S' shaped meat hook, with a potato on the sharp bottom end to save your hand from being stabbed when you reached for a piece.

The top end of the 'S' hook was conveniently hung on the closest available place.

Now, thinking of the ultra-soft, imagine this chunk of newspaper and how thick and non-absorbent it was, plus it was stiff.

The first order of the day was to scrunch it up, and try to make it as wrinkly and soft as possible before applying it to tender parts of your anatomy.

This was not always a success, especially as the over-inked papers had a habit of shedding their ink onto your gluteus maximus!

Aside from this, some homeowners I am convinced, were masochists.

They would provide a wad of toilet paper made from GLOSSY MAGAZINES!

Miséricorde! Can you just imagine? Hard, slick and glossy!

Oh, what a predicament; paper burns where it doesn't show!

I always had nasty thoughts for the homeowners, where I visited that had toilet paper like this.

So now, today, I will happily take ANY modern toilet paper and gladly enjoy the advances in technology that have rid us of the squares of magazine on the 'S' hook—thank goodness for modern society.